petal&

twig

Helleborus argutifolius

petal &
twig

Seasonal Bouquets *with* Blossoms, Branches, *and* Grasses *from* Your Garden

VALERIE EASTON

SASQUATCH BOOKS
SEATTLE

*To my family, for their encouragement and support,
especially my daughter, Katie, who had a hand in this book. And to my
dog, Bridget, who keeps me company while I write and garden.*

Published by Sasquatch Books
17 16 15 14 13 12   9 8 7 6 5 4 3 2 1

Front and back cover photographs: Kathryn Barnard
Cover and interior design: Anna Goldstein
Interior photographs: Valerie Easton (except pages vi, 16, 98, and 112, copyright © Allan Mandell;
    and page 22, copyright © Katie Easton)
Interior map by Katie Easton
Interior composition: Anna Goldstein

Library of Congress Cataloging-in-Publication Data
Easton, Valerie.
  Petal and twig : seasonal bouquets with blossoms, branches, and grasses from your
garden / Valerie Easton.
     p. cm.
  Includes bibliographical references.
  ISBN 978-1-57061-766-9 (alk. paper)
1. Bouquets. 2. Gardening. I. Title.
  SB449.5.B65E27 2012
  745.92--dc23
                              2011026020

Sasquatch Books
119 South Main Street, Suite 400
Seattle, WA 98104
(206) 467-4300
www.sasquatchbooks.com
custserv@sasquatchbooks.com

contents

Hardy fuchsias, and mophead and 'Annabelle' hydrangeas, ready to be picked by mid-August in my garden on Whidbey Island.

introduction

*If we could see the miracle of a single flower,
our whole life would change.*

—THE BUDDHA

Simple bouquets are all about the joy of cutting flowers and foliage from our gardens and bringing them inside, not about decorating or accessorizing the house.

Most books on flower arranging have oddly little to do with gardens. Their elaborate floral constructions have even less to do with our busy and informal lives. I'm always amazed at how designers and florists manage to take the nature out of nature.

Sometimes it's easiest to define something by what it is not. This little book isn't about wiring or manipulating plant materials, interior decorating, or impressing guests. It's simply about taking a delight in flowers, leaves, and what nature offers up.

If we're intimidated by the grandiosity of flower arranging, all that fragrant, soul-stirring beauty will stay outdoors, rather than grace our indoor lives as well as our gardens.

For most gardeners, the simple act of cutting what they find beautiful or interesting in their gardens and bringing it into their houses is all about their love of plant life. What chance do we have of realizing the Buddha's miracle of a single flower if we distort or manipulate plants so that they no longer express their own essence?

This book is all about how easy, fun, and creatively satisfying flower arranging can be. I'd even suggest that the simpler and more spontaneous you keep the process of cutting and arranging, the more happiness you'll find in it. All you need do is go outdoors with an open mind, a pair of sharp clippers, and the willingness to look closely. Arrange as much as you'd like, or better yet, plop your bouquet, handheld and fresh from the garden, into a vase and call it good.

Organic gardeners have peace of mind setting a bouquet of sweet peas freshly cut from the backyard on the counter where their children eat breakfast. Nothing is more local and seasonal than flowers and foliage grown right outside your own back door. Who wants to worry about flowers doused in chemicals or the environmental cost of raising flowers in hothouses and shipping them across countries, oceans, and continents? Consider this crazy number—80 percent of the cut flowers sold in the United States are imported. It's time we extend our thinking about safety, organic practices, and localism to the flowers we bring into our homes, put on our tables, and set by our bedsides.

Although hothouse flowers can certainly be showier, there's great gratification in growing each bloom yourself. You've watered your flowers' roots and watched your plants stretch toward the sun. You've known each blossom since it was a seed or a start just pushing out of the soil. You live the history of bouquets from your own garden, which makes arranging them a focused act of intimacy.

Admiring small, handmade bouquets and catching a whiff of their fresh or perfumed scent as you go about cooking, eating, reading, and working are such pleasures. The silkiness of their petals, the exuberance of leaves and stamen, all tell the story of tending the soil, of what the weather has been like over the last weeks, of dewy mornings, chilly evenings, warm afternoons.

If flowers are distilled emotion, then gathering and combining them into a single arrangement is surely the most expressive of arts. Choosing which ones to bring indoors and cutting and combining them in various patterns and colors is one more expression of our love for our gardens and what we grow there. We live with our plants when we're outside; why not when we're inside, where we can enjoy them many more hours of the day and into the evenings? Raising vegetables and fruit offers many of the same pleasures, with the additional satisfaction of cooking and eating, but then they're gone. Cut early in the morning and arranged gently, flowers will usually last a week in the house.

Then there's the zen of flower arranging, which can be a sweet little oasis of beauty and calm in the midst of a hectic day. Working with flowers is thoroughly absorbing once you find the pace of it. A little music and a cup of tea help slow you down to closely consider the possibilities. Whether you're gathering a simple nosegay of pansies and plunking it into a tin or working with a larger mixed bunch, take your time. After all, you're crafting performance art that changes hour by hour, day by day, as buds open, petals drop, and flowers droop. Imperfection engages us in the creative process. The ephemeral nature of bouquets makes them even more precious. Soon enough, they'll be wilted flowers in stinky water, ready to be tossed into the compost.

Which brings us back to the garden, where it all starts. A big part of a garden's enduring fascination is how it expresses the seasons. I look forward all year to certain plants leafing out and others blooming. A white jug filled with deep-purple lilacs, forsythia forced into bright flower in darkest winter, or a basket overflowing with moss and French pink pussy willows, are events that mark the seasons in a more heartfelt, sensory way than the calendar can.

Which is why arranging materials from the garden, rather than buying out-of-season flowers, is so satisfying. We can celebrate and even exaggerate the seasons indoors. Spring flowers are so stunning and often so exquisitely fragrant that a bouquet of lilacs or mock orange is perfection. In summer, you're inundated with happy choices. A mass of blooms in a single color can look brilliant, or the overwhelming bounty of the summer garden can be gathered into lush, scented bouquets of lilies and roses. The mellow colors of autumn, with berries and vegetables mixed in, can be an expression of both the harvest and the days growing shorter and colder. Winter bouquets are more about shape and line of bare branches or the endurance of evergreens. It's a time to celebrate the somber colors and remember that brown, gray, and green are magnificent in their own earthy way, especially when viewed in their textural splendor close up in a vase.

Arranging flowers through the seasons offers concentrated lessons in design that can shape you into becoming a more thoughtful and acute gardener. I can't tell you how many times I've moved plants around in the garden based on some pleasing combination I've discovered in the vase but never noticed out there in the dirt. Imagination is as important to this process as sharp clippers. Soon enough, you'll be happily picturing possible bouquets when you plant seeds, bulbs, starts, and plants. And you'll be looking at flowers and foliage you've cut for the vase, seeing new color and textural possibilities, then running outside with a shovel to rearrange plants in the garden.

Nearly forty years ago, I started gardening to have flowers for the house. My love of bringing the garden inside turned me into a gardener, which in turn informed my planting over the years. It launched me into a career of horticultural librarianship as well as writing stories, books, and blogs about plants and gardens.

All these years of gardening, cutting, arranging, and living with flowers has remained a keen and personal pleasure. Cutting and bringing the garden indoors in all seasons distills its essence so we can better appreciate and play around with all the possibilities, indoors and out.

Allium 'Globemaster', *Allium* 'Purple Sensation', and *Spirea japonica* 'Magic Carpet' in May.

elements, practicalities, style, and color

To me, flower arranging involves a lot more than flowers, and much more than arranging, but I can't find a better name for it.

—EDWINA VON GAL IN *FRESH CUTS*

ELEMENTS

Flowers are a plant's sexual parts. We're attracted to their colors, shapes, and sweet scents just as the bees and butterflies are. But flowers are fleeting; once they've performed their reproductive duty, a plant no longer needs to put all that energy into producing such beauty. What you're left with—foliage, bark, twig, stem, fruit, seedpod, and branch—all have their charms. To enjoy both your garden and bouquets year-round, it pays to get over flowers and appreciate plants' more subtle offerings of texture, shape, and form.

Buds

Buds hold all the promise of spring in their closed-up-tight potential. How can such small packages contain all the leaves, flowers, and twigs for the coming year? Buds vary greatly in size, shape, and texture; some are fuzzy, while others are bumpy or silky. No matter their surface, all buds are dramatic as they slowly crack open, often changing color as they teasingly unfurl the petals inside.

It's as if the slow, slow silent opening dance of buds plays on our longing for spring. They increase our sense of anticipation by drawing out their time on center stage. Sometimes buds themselves are the main show, as with the sweet, gray furriness of pussy willows and the tight coil of fern fronds. Other times, buds may be thrilling but soon forgotten when they pop open to reveal flowers as gorgeous and fragrant as magnolia blooms.

Magnolia 'Elizabeth'

Seedpods

From pinecones to the striped, round puffballs left behind when nigella's blue blossoms fall, late summer and autumn are the weeks and months to gather these textural wonders. They can be piled in bowls, lined up on a windowsill, or left on stems and branches as eye-catching elements in a bouquet, as with the silvery, moon-like pods of the old-fashioned money plant (*Lunaria annua*).

Seed Heads

These wonderful little additions to bouquets, whether cut from ornamental grasses, pasqueflowers, or clematis, usually start out with silky filaments that turn to fluffy puffs. Because they don't last very long, I've rarely seen seed heads for sale; they are among those special bits you need to grow yourself to enrich your bouquets. Best of all, you just come across them as the garden ages, nodding atop what used to be an alpina clematis flower, now a whole new little curiosity.

Berries

Many plants that we think of for their flowers, like roses and viburnum, give a second season of interest when they fruit. Fat, red and orange rose hips, the ethereally pale-green berries or the shiny black ones on mahonias, and the metallic lavender fruit on callicarpa, are every bit as eye-catching as most flowers and are especially welcome in autumn when not many flowers are blooming anyway. And don't forget to swipe a few canes and stems of fruit like raspberries, blueberries, and tomatoes, all of which look great in bouquets as well as served for dinner or dessert.

Branches and Twigs

They may be the bones of the garden, what's left behind in winter, but the varying textures, colors, and graphic shapes of branches and twigs bring height, drama, and line to the vase. Red and yellow twig dogwood, coral bark Japanese maple, and ghost brambles (*Rubus thibetanus* 'Silver Fern') are intensely colored in winter. Just about any bare branch can be clipped to lend an interesting line to an arrangement. Boughs of broadleaf evergreens like magnolias and camellia, or conifers like pine and cypress, plump up bouquets with their texture and bring the fresh, tangy scent of winter into the house.

PRACTICALITIES

Cutting

If you're one of the many gardeners afraid of ruining your garden's looks and even health by cutting its bounty, here's a mantra for you: It's okay to alter the shape of plants, remove a few flowers, and generally plunder the place—it's your garden, after all, and it benefits from being thinned a bit.

When done with care, cutting improves the look of plants while allowing more light and air circulation into the garden. Many plants continue to bloom only if you keep cutting. If you slack off on regularly clipping roses, pansies, sweet peas, and bleeding heart, the plants move on to their next life stage and you're out of flowers for the season.

Perhaps the biggest benefit to the garden is how closely you pay attention to your plants when you're out there cutting for bouquets. While you pause, shears in hand, to contemplate colors, textures, and line, you can't help but notice what's going on. As you stretch to pluck a rosebud or duck beneath a shrub to cut a crossing branch, you see which plants are struggling with disease or pests and which are being squeezed by their neighbors or leaning toward the sun so much they'd benefit from a transplant. Mostly, you just tune in to which plants might need a little extra water, space, staking, or general attention.

A few commonsense guidelines to help you cut effectively, safely, and unobtrusively:

❊ Cut early in the cool of the morning, when flowers are freshest. What better excuse to get outside and enjoy your garden first thing in the morning?

❊ Always cut so as not to disfigure the plant.

❊ Start by clipping branches or stems that have been broken, are trailing on the ground, sticking out at odd angles, or that cross or rub on other branches.

❊ Avoid cutting next year's buds on plants like peonies and hydrangeas.

❊ Remember the whole garden offers up cutting possibilities, and spread your plundering about. If you cut from trees and shrubs as well as flowers, from raised beds, hedges, and pots, no one plant or area of the garden will be greatly reduced.

❊ If you're allergic to sap or if you're dealing with thorny plants like roses or quince, wear heavy gloves to protect your flesh and clothes.

Keeping Flowers Fresh

Once you've made the cut, plunge freshly severed stems into tepid (not cold) water as soon as possible. Toting a basket or trug around the garden with you while cutting may be picturesque, but it's better for the flowers if you have a water-filled bucket close by so the cut flowers can be plunged right in and start hydrating as soon as they've been picked.

Your flowers will last longer if you have an hour or so to let them rest in a cool, shady spot—a garage, carport, or under a big tree is ideal—before putting them in a vase. But if you're eager to get arranging, go ahead, it doesn't really matter very much.

A cut flower's ability to drink water determines how long it will last. Crush or split woody stems, and recut all stems right before arranging. (It takes only a minute or two of dryness for the stem ends to scale over so that they are unable to drink.)

Flowers are resilient. Cutting in the cool of the morning keeps flowers fresher longer, but if you're inspired to run outside on a warm afternoon and clip a quick bouquet, that's good too. So often spontaneous arrangements give the most pleasure, even if they last a shorter time than if you follow all the steps.

I'm not convinced using a preservative really prolongs a bouquet's life span significantly, but when I'm putting together a big bouquet, or when the weather is especially warm, I sometimes mix up the old-fashioned home-made floral preservative that follows. It does keep the water from getting slimy and stinky, which makes emptying the vase at the end of a week or so a more pleasant chore.

For the floral preservative, mix together:

    3 cups water
    1 tablespoon sugar
    1 teaspoon vinegar
    1 crushed aspirin

Arranging

Once you start in with the wires and tape and other floristry paraphernalia, you're manipulating rather than working with a plant's natural attributes. You don't need to fix a flower or transform it into some ideal. Wire and tape rob plants of their organic look. Just as a bad staking job in the garden makes a plant look stiff and unfortunately military, so do wired flowers lose a sense of life and movement. Put up with a little flopping, and your bouquets will benefit.

As with pie dough, leaves, stems, and flowers are best handled as little as possible. Touch your materials only briefly—your goal is to get the plants plopped into the vase and slurping water.

Making a bouquet can be as easy as sticking flowers loosely into a container so that you can see the special character of each. All you need are sharp clippers, fresh water, a watertight vessel, and a thoughtful, appreciative eye. We don't need to treat flower arranging as a ceremony, but it helps to acknowledge that working with nature is an art form rich in spirit, inventiveness, and appreciation. Sometimes a little ritual around the work does just that.

Strip or cut all lower leaves off every stem because you don't want any foliage beneath the water line in the vase. Clean, stripped stems keep the water as clean as possible, and the flowers fresher longer. Sometimes as I take off leaves, I see how much better the flower looks sans foliage (as with tulips); go ahead and remove all the foliage if you like how that looks. It can be fun to try sticking foliage from a different plant or plants altogether in there—it's your bouquet, after all.

When you recut stems to the right length for the vase, cut them at an angle so they absorb as much water as possible. Use a hammer to crush or mangle the bottom inch or so of woody stems like those of red twig dogwood, lilac, or mock orange. For hellebores, split the stems up an inch or so to encourage them to keep drinking water. To keep "bleeders" like poppies and euphorbia fresh longer, singe the bottom of each stem with a match or a lighter for a few seconds until it turns brown.

Ongoing Care

Top off vases with cool water every day or so. You'll be amazed at how quickly some bouquets drink water.

If the flowers flop, you can revive them by recutting stem ends and refilling the vase with fresh, cool water.

STYLE

Leonardo Da Vinci said, "Simplicity is the ultimate sophistication," and this is especially true for bouquets. When you're dealing with materials that by their nature are luscious, colorful, and vital, the less you intervene the better.

We don't really need to work hard to arrange flowers because we can simply place them in a pleasing manner, in their most natural form, into vessels that enhance their beauty. Think of it this way: we can't really improve on nature—just display it thoughtfully and sensitively. You don't need any special training or talent—just an honest eye, a willingness to observe what's growing right outside your door, and the time to play around with the possibilities. The art of making bouquets lies in your readiness to respond in the moment to what is growing right outside your door, cut flowers and foliage that appeal to you, and combine them in ways that look right at that moment.

You especially don't need to ponder whether you're a minimalist or prefer English cottage-style bouquets stuffed with colorful blooms. Some days, a big mixed bouquet might look ridiculously overblown; on other days and in other seasons it might lift your spirits and be just right. Look to your materials and your mood on any given day. It depends on how you feel, what vase appeals, and most of all what cuttings you have in your hand. When I worked as a librarian, we were always told to catalog the book we had in our hand, not some past edition or other possible version. This immediacy of dealing with just what you have before you applies to arranging flowers, too. Work with what you have.

Much depends on where you plan to place the bouquet in your home. You can start out with a spot in mind and cut and arrange to suit that spot. Or you can be inspired by the garden and figure out where your bouquet should go once you've created it. But a giant, fluffy bouquet in the center of the dining room table isn't a good idea if anyone is going to sit down and eat there. And you don't want to display tiny, delicate treasures on a huge chest where they'll look dwarfed or where no one can come close enough to see them. I have favorite spots in my house for bouquets—by the bed when I have fragrant flowers to cut, always in the guest bath when I have company coming, and on the kitchen island or windowsill where I see them most often.

If you're working with colors you love as you cut and arrange, you won't go wrong. Step back sometimes to look at mass and form. Blur your eyes to get the overall effect. As with accessories, when something doesn't look quite right, you're better off removing it instead of adding more material in an attempt to fix it. If a bouquet doesn't please your eye, try taking things out rather than stuffing more in. If you can practice the difficult art of not-too-much, especially challenging in late spring and early summer when the garden is exploding with possibilities, you're likely to end up with a bouquet that pleases you. The exception to the less-is-more rule is when an arrangement cries out for more foliage. Adding leaves can often mediate between competing flowers and settle a bouquet into harmony.

Whenever I find myself having a Martha Stewart perfectionist moment, I remember the Japanese art of *wabi sabi*, which elevates imperfection, messiness, decline, and decay to an art form. It's all about the nature of change and humble materials, which pretty much defines flower arranging from the garden. Wabi sabi finds sweetness in restraint and satisfaction in simplicity—and so will you if you can leave your bouquet alone enough to be just what it is.

The most comforting thing about wabi sabi is the idea that blemishes and irregularities are good things that bestow character and ensure modesty. This attitude helps keep flower arranging a subtle and intimate art. Other wabi sabi principles, such as attention to detail and an aim for simplicity and balance, serve the bouquet maker well.

This bouquet is all about color contrasts, with the intensity of the deep-blue iris set off by orange geum and chartreuse euphorbia.

COLOR

Picasso contemplated color his entire, long life and still believed it to be a great mystery. Gardens are all about color, and this carries through into the vase. Color is more a vibratory experience than merely a visual sense. Watermelon pink shimmers out an atmosphere of heat; cool blue grasses create shivers. If we're receptive, color douses us in memory and emotion.

It's often said the mark of a sophisticated gardener is an acute appreciation of the color green. But even with this most pervasive of nature's colors, we're still talking about a variety of shades and nuances. Green is lime, chartreuse, forest, emerald, moss, gray-green, and blue-green in glorious tints and tones. Even an all-white garden or bouquet is about gradations of blush, cream, snow, frost, and all the other shades of pale.

Cottage gardens are beloved for their seemingly artless mix of vivid flower colors. Such random and lively use of color gladdens our hearts. Don't we react to books by the color on their covers (or lack of it)? And even if we prefer to wear taupe or black, we always turn our heads to look at a woman in a bright-red dress. Does anyone want to dig into a plate of gray or beige food? No matter how modern, stylish, or minimalist we are in our general tastes and in particular gardens and bouquets, the very timber of our nervous system quivers in response to color. That's why I refuse to believe that dogs are color blind—how could they be such joyous creatures without the ability to see color?

Nothing is more personal than color, so don't be intimidated about playing around with it to find what you love best. Color is subjective and pliable, changeable and thrilling. You need color sensitivity, not color expertise (whatever that is) to make satisfying bouquets.

There's no magic formula or recipe for color, but rather close observation and the willingness to experiment. And colors change, depending on a flower or leaf's maturation, the time of day and year, and especially the weather. Sun, rain, and clouds, morning, afternoon, or evening light all alter your perceptions—just wait a few minutes and the colors look different.

Most of us don't have the self-restraint of Georgia O'Keeffe, who said of a particularly productive period in her life, "I began with charcoal and paper and decided not to use any color until it was impossible to do what I wanted to do in black and white. . . . I believe it was June before I needed blue." The French painter Rousseau was asked once why he put a naked woman on a red sofa in the middle of one of his jungle paintings. "I needed a bit of red there," he answered.

One of the most freeing things to learn about color, in addition to the idea you can dab it about anywhere you need a bit of red, is that color is all about relationships. In bouquets, flowers and leaves are in such close proximity that each exerts great influence on the other. Also, the amount of color matters—a dab is very different in intensity and effect than a slab. If you're ever not quite sure how you feel about whatever color play you've concocted, add more leaves. Foliage is the great arbitrator, with an uncanny ability to calm and soothe cantankerous colors. Whether green, variegated, gold, or purple, foliage makes all the difference in how flower colors play off one another in the vase and in the ground.

Trust your eye and your own sense of color, play around with it, and stay open to the possibility of loving pink when you never did before or noticing nuances you never believed existed in a color as obvious as red. If you're willing to tap into your moods, memories, and emotions to appreciate color, you'll also tap into the great color mystery that holds within it so much of the passion, drama, joy, and satisfaction of flower arranging.

Oriental lilies, dark-leafed ligularia, raspberries, and sweet peas behind them, in raised beds in the early August garden.

the world as your cutting garden

Too often, we fail to make the connection between our gardens, the greater outside world, and flowers for the house. But there's no reason the outside should stay put and even less reason to think of flowers as something to be ordered by phone or picked up with the groceries.

A flower arranger's most useful skill has nothing to do with wielding a pair of sharp clippers. Most valuable is the ability and willingness to open your eyes to all that's growing in your garden and in the world around you. It's the pleasure of seeing and considering the moss on a nearby fence, the weeds in the ditch, herbs you bring inside for dinner, and every part of every plant you grow. With this fresh and unbounded vision, it's possible to fashion bouquets most weeks of the year from even the tiniest garden and exercise your creativity and sense of possibility at the same time.

When you see the whole wide world as a cutting and gathering garden, you'll notice horse chestnuts split from their spiny shells and lying on the ground in autumn. You'll appreciate how conveniently your neighbors' just-opening cherry blossoms hang over your fence. Even if they never ripen enough to eat, you'll see the beauty in green cherry tomatoes cascading down the side of a vase. Even when a ligularia's flowers are long past, and its huge leaves have collapsed in a heap, the fuzzy seed heads are an intriguing, eye-catching addition to bouquets. It is impossible to buy, at any price, such freshness or diversity of flower, fruit, and foliage. In the quest for materials to fill a vase, everything from groundcovers to trees, from vegetables to grasses, is fair game.

A few years ago, I downsized gardens from an overplanted suburban quarter acre to a 2,400-square-foot plot in the village of Langley, on Whidbey Island. Much of the garden space is taken up by deck, terraces, pathways, and raised beds. To make the most of the space, I thought about the warm, walled area around many English houses, used for growing food and flowers and for sitting and dining al fresco. Outside these sheltering walls lay the rest of the estate. I skipped the estate part and emulated the intimate garden closely connected to the house, using modern materials rather than old brick walls. And from this cozy, confined space, I can fill a vase or two in most weeks of the year. Hellebores, poppies, sweet peas, clematis, euphorbia, and little shrubs like daphne and colorful spirea are my go-tos for vase fodder, used again and again in different combinations to brighten the house with color and perfume. And don't forget fruit, vegetables, and herbs; bronze fennel plumps out a bouquet, and blueberry branches add autumnal color. The world outside your fence and a lush garden within it, planted thickly enough to hide the effect of all the clipping, is the only way to have such luxury.

TRADE, PILLAGE, AND PLUNDER

No need to confine yourself to your own garden. Carrying home something that catches your eye on a walk and trading blooms with neighbors adds to the bounty and the fun. Gardeners have long traded seeds and starts—why not flowers and foliage? In this era of shrinking properties and lower-maintenance gardens, it doesn't make sense for every garden on your street, or every one of your gardening friends, to devote space to quince, mock orange, or forsythia. Why don't we all give precious garden space to what we love best, then do a little swapping over the backyard fence? I can't tell you how often I've approached neighbors with some fresh fruit, cut branches, or flowers in hand, and asked whether in turn I could cut a lilac in a color I don't grow myself, or a few stems of rainbow chard, or whatever I don't have happening in my own garden at the moment.

I admit I often take a bag and clippers along with me on a walk and return home with some choice bit for the vase. I'm always pleased that I suffered the embarrassment of walking the dog with pruners in hand. But always practice good garden ethics by asking before you cut on someone else's property. Admire, but don't cut, plants growing in public parks or other public areas that are there for everyone to enjoy. Plants growing over the fence onto your property are yours for the cutting, as long as you respect the marauder's health and looks. When you're out and about and foraging, the rule of thumb is never to remove or take away more than 10 percent of any single plant or any plant population. Always cut to further a plant's health and beauty; strive to leave little or no evidence of your pruning.

Val Easton's 2,400-square-foot garden on Whidbey Island

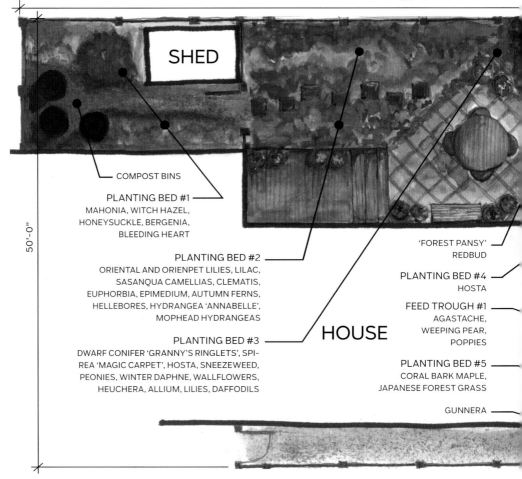

80'-0"

50'-0"

SHED

COMPOST BINS

PLANTING BED #1
MAHONIA, WITCH HAZEL,
HONEYSUCKLE, BERGENIA,
BLEEDING HEART

PLANTING BED #2
ORIENTAL AND ORIENPET LILIES, LILAC,
SASANQUA CAMELLIAS, CLEMATIS,
EUPHORBIA, EPIMEDIUM, AUTUMN FERNS,
HELLEBORES, HYDRANGEA 'ANNABELLE',
MOPHEAD HYDRANGEAS

PLANTING BED #3
DWARF CONIFER 'GRANNY'S RINGLETS', SPI-
REA 'MAGIC CARPET', HOSTA, SNEEZEWEED,
PEONIES, WINTER DAPHNE, WALLFLOWERS,
HEUCHERA, ALLIUM, LILIES, DAFFODILS

HOUSE

'FOREST PANSY'
REDBUD

PLANTING BED #4
HOSTA

FEED TROUGH #1
AGASTACHE,
WEEPING PEAR,
POPPIES

PLANTING BED #5
CORAL BARK MAPLE,
JAPANESE FOREST GRASS

GUNNERA

PLANTING BED #6
'WESTERLAND' ROSE, SWEET PEAS, CLEMATIS

GOLDEN LOCUST

FEED TROUGH #2
DWARF POLE APPLE, ALSTROEMERIA, TULIPS

FEED TROUGH #3
AGAPANTHUS, CONEFLOWER, GEUM

FEED TROUGH #4
STRAWBERRIES, PUMPKINS, GALLARDIA

BAMBOO HEDGE

RAISED BED #1
LILIES, HERBS, BRONZE FENNEL

RAISED BED #2
ROSEMARY, CERINTHE, CROCOSMIA, PASQUEFLOWER

RAISED BED #3
LETTUCE, CAREX, LIGULARIA

RAISED BED #4
RASPBERRIES, LAVENDER, NIGELA, POPPIES

RAISED BED #5
DAHLIAS, SWEET PEAS, KALE, 'RAINBOW LIGHTS' CHARD, ARTICHOKES

RAISED BED #6
DELPHINIUM, LAVENDER, LILIES

Is it a lizard? A frog? A patterned Mexican pitcher adds personality to this springtime bouquet.

petal & twig
containers

As with earrings or shoes, it seems that you can never have too many vases. No matter how many I've collected over the years, from raku to jam jars and tea tins, I often picture something a little different as I hold a bouquet in my hand, considering which container might suit best. What perversity is this? It's a comfort that I love the vases I've had for years as much as my latest find.

Often it's a vase that inspires a bouquet with its color, finish, or shape. Just the thought of purple hydrangeas massed in a yellow pitcher makes me salivate for summer. I crave the moment in autumn when the leaves turn just the right shade of gold to look perfect in a claret-colored urn. In spring, tiny, clear vases show off delicate snowdrops, crocus, and miniature daffodils. In autumn, tall, earthy jugs are sturdy enough to hold boughs and branches safely.

If you collect containers in a variety of sizes, styles, and finishes you love, you'll always have something suitable at hand. Choose what you like best and you'll enjoy looking at your vases when they're empty, which of course they will be more of the time than not.

Keep an open mind as to what makes a good vase—many vessels intended for the kitchen, like wine glasses, bowls and pitchers, make interesting, versatile containers. Any container that holds water securely qualifies as a vase; and even this definition is flexible because baskets and other porous containers can be lined with jars or water glasses.

The most important thing is to collect all manner of vases that appeal to you, so you'll feel inspired to make bouquets. Maybe some people can limit their vases to a precious few that always suit their arrangements. But I love the possibilities and provocation to creativity that come with having lots of options.

Changes of season require different kinds of vases. The garden and your eye change with the light, temperature, and weather. In spring, simple clear vases, ones in colored glass and pale, matte colors show off the sea-and-sky shades of that fresh season. Summer bouquets need strongly shaped and vividly colored containers. You need big pitchers and jugs to hold summer's sunflowers and lilies.

In autumn, vases that are metallic, burnished, glossy, and satisfyingly plump all play off the matte quality of leaf and needle that predominate as the gardening year winds down. In winter, when the pickings are skimpy, vases with architectural shapes, rich colors, and striking textures keep things interesting.

Where to store all those vases? I envy people with special sinks to arrange flowers and a room full of shelves to organize their vases. But you don't need special equipment or lots of space for flower arranging. My kitchen counter and sink work just fine. I painted an old cabinet Chinese red with the palest, icy-blue interior to store my vases where I can enjoy the sight of them whether or not they're holding flowers.

All you need, really, are plenty of vases you love close at hand to create that lovely synergy between flowers and container that results in the most satisfying bouquets.

An old cupboard painted coral outside and ice blue inside to display vases when they're not in use.

Pasqueflower, tulips, lilac, and euphorbia in a May bouquet.

bouquet journal

All the sensuality, symbolism, and sheer beauty of the garden is magnified indoors, where a single twig of *Daphne odora* perfumes an entire room, hydrangeas drying in a vase evoke the warmth of long summer days, and the pungency and bristle of an evergreen branch remind us that nature is enduring out there even when the weather is at its nastiest.

Because my garden is so small, I've used leaves, flowers, and branches from the same plants over and over again in bouquets through the weeks and even months. I'm continually surprised at how different these materials look in various combinations and vases. Figuring out how to make the most out of what I have room to grow is a big part of the fun. It's like cooking from the refrigerator and cupboards rather than running to the store when you can't figure out what to make for dinner.

Thank goodness for stalwarts like euphorbia, epimedium, hydrangeas, and dahlias. The creativity involved in thinking up new combinations and switching out vases is gratifying because the effort helps you see familiar plants in new ways. This experience then translates into your gardening life outdoors as well.

Every bit of material you see in these bouquets is gathered from my own little backyard garden in Langley, traded with neighbors, or scavenged from roadsides or alleys within a few blocks of home. I had a blast photographing what I was arranging in most weeks of the year; many of the photos are taken in our Langley house and garden. I commute from Langley to Seattle every week, bringing flowers and vegetables back to the city, and in some cases, I photographed the bouquets in our Seattle condo.

So here we go—bouquets from a Northwest garden in most weeks of the year. Let's start with the spring equinox, when the garden is just waking up and the earth tilts so that the days and nights are of equal length.

SPRING

Spring truly arrives, no matter what the date, temperature, or drizzle, when I can go outside, usually the first week of April, and cut armfuls of flowers to bring in to fill a whole line-up of vases. For the first time since the dahlias faded in October, fresh flowers fill the house.

Spring flowers are so exquisite in their delicacy, fragrance, and sea-and-sky washed colors that in springtime, more than in any other season, less is more. In this surge of verdancy lies the challenge—it is so tempting to create riotous, multicolored displays. Sometimes a great, big mixed bouquet is just the thing, but I'm afraid too often it looks as if it belongs in a hotel lobby rather than a home.

The art lies in the edit; a sculptor speaks of whittling away stone to reveal what exists inside. The essence of springtime is best captured with a single parrot tulip, the line of an azalea branch, or the tender unfurling of a fern frond. Such restraint is especially difficult this time of year when the garden is exploding with temptations.

Try three white peonies in a glass vase, with their own fine foliage, for a stunningly simple arrangement. Or strip all the leaves from branches of a single kind of rhododendron, and arrange the flowers in a low bowl. What could look better than a blue jug brimming with pale daffodils? Or if you want to use lots of different kinds of flowers, try sticking each in a little glass vase by itself, and then cluster the vases together; this creates impact while offering you the chance to appreciate each exquisite blossom. What could be prettier and smell better than a tumbler full of lily of the valley? Or you can dig up a clump and stick it, soil and all, in a shallow dish, where it will bloom happily indoors for weeks, spreading its sweet perfume about the house.

Don't overlook the small trees in your garden as vase material. Branches coated with cherry, plum, and crab apple flowers make fluffy bouquets, as pretty when half the blossoms are strewn all over the table as when they are freshly cut. Then there are the flowering shrubs like lilac, daphne, mock orange, rhododendron, exbury azalea, and Korean spice viburnum.

Mix in plenty of foliage—leaves are never as glowingly chartreuse as when they first unfold. The soothing green diffuses the clash of brightly colored blossoms.

Vines with their grasping tendrils capture the buzz of springtime energy, their drape and curl adding a distinct element to any arrangement. *Clematis armandii* lends sweetly perfumed, white or pale pink flowers and pliable new bronze foliage. I use it in every bouquet for at least a month, beginning when it opens its first flower in February. *Akebia quinata* has dramatic leaves and tiny flowers of great sweetness, and the little sky-blue bells of *Clematis alpina* are as beguiling dangling down the side of a vase as they are decorating a tree or arbor.

Now that the garden is really going, and there are so many flowers and fresh foliage to choose from, it's best not to overthink a bouquet. Just go outdoors, look around, and cut what strikes you. Choose one strong element like a peony, or even a favorite vase, and build around it.

Every garden and bouquet depend upon the chorus girls of springtime—peonies, magnolias, fat cottage tulips, hyacinths, and camellia. Even used sparingly, these blowsy beauties are over-the-top showstoppers. The springtime garden builds from delicate narcissus poking up from the soil in March to an unsurpassed riot of color and scent by the time of the summer solstice.

❋

March 20

It's a windy, warm, 68 degrees F on the south end of Whidbey Island on the first day of spring. I am buzzed by a hummingbird out in the garden, I can see baby lambs and their freshly shorn mamas in the pastures across the street, and the garden is full of cheery narcissus.

I grow the most sweetly scented, warmest colored narcissus I can find, and plant as many as I can squeeze in. I love how the golden and orange tones warm up chilly spring days. Not much else is fragrant yet out there, and the warm colors play beautifully off all the springtime blues and pastels.

A simple glass vase holds a fat bunch of orange-trimmed daffodils, including 'Falconet', a favorite for its sweet perfume and bright color;

'Bantam', which is sturdy and dependable; 'Serola', a pretty combo of amber and orange and a dependable perennializer; and 'Ceylon' with its buttercup-yellow petals. I try to plant mostly early to midspring bloomers because early is the point of daffodils (except for a few irresistibly fragrant Pheasant's Eye types like 'Recurvus', which bloom later).

Narcissus 'Bantam', 'Serola', 'Falconet', 'Ceylon'

Bleeding heart (*Dicentra spectabilis* 'Gold Heart')

Euphorbia 'Red Martin'

The daffodils look fine all by themselves, but I couldn't resist tucking in some burgundy euphorbia and a few floppy leaves and pink flower sprays of bleeding heart. This newer variety of an old-fashioned favorite has chartreuse leaves and peach-colored stems. Like many old-fashioned flowers, it grows stronger and blooms more generously the more you cut it.

❋

March 26

A week later, Pheasant's Eye type daffodils are blooming along with a purple hellebore and dark-purple hyacinth, inspiring this intensely fragrant arrangement. The bleeding heart foliage has grown large enough, and the hellebore is pretty enough, that the daffodils are no longer the stars of the show. Yet they stand out for their winged shape, exquisite eye, sweet scent, and for how their petals echo the pale, matte vase.

The spicy daffodils and supremely sweet hyacinths perfume the entire room. The soft, droopy leaves of the bleeding heart are supported by the upright stance of the hyacinths. A few, dark hellebores are tucked in; they will slowly open during the week if the stems are split an inch or two to help them drink water and stay fresh.

Daffodils (*Narcissus poeticus* var. *recurvus*)

Helleborus x *hybridus*

Bleeding heart (*Dicentra spectabilis* 'Gold Heart')

Hyacinth 'Peter Stuyvesant'

April 2

I pick flowers in near gale-force winds and sleeting rain a couple of days before Easter. It's so chilly that the lilacs aren't quite ready yet, but I'm so eager for their scent that I cut a few to watch and sniff as the buds open in the warmth of the house. The hellebores are at their peak, and the Korean spice viburnum buds open enough to exude their spicy-sweet fragrance. This and the snowball viburnum, draping the side of the vase, need their stems sliced open a few inches, and they last longer if they sit in warmish water a bit before you arrange them.

The orange tulips, just going over, add a jolt of color, echoed by the bronze, springtime foliage of 'Magic Carpet' spirea. I tuck in pink bleeding heart to sweeten the bouquet for Easter, and I gather the lavender and purple flowers of money plant (*Lunaria annua*), which grows wild in a nearby alley. Be sure to strip the big, lax leaves from this vigorous biennial because they tend to obscure the pretty little flowers. No color sophistication here— just a blend of springtime fireworks that prove orange and pink combine beautifully when refereed by chartreuse. Also the simple, chalky white cylinder of a vase lowers the temperature a bit.

The *wulfenii* euphorbia (a.k.a. Mediterranean spurge) needs to be handled carefully because its sap is poisonous and can cause a bad rash if you're sensitive to it. Wear gloves when you cut it, and wash your hands right away after working with it. Because the sap bleeds right out of the stem, causing it to wilt, you need to singe the bottom of the stem after cutting—I do this with one of those long candle lighters. Just hold the flame to the bottom of

Tulip 'Orange Queen'

Korean spice viburnum (*Viburnum carlesii* 'Compactum')

Money plant (*Lunaria annua*)

Snowball bush (*Viburnum opulus* 'Sterile')

Euphorbia characias, spp. *wulfenii*

Spirea japonica 'Magic Carpet'

Lilac (*Syringa vulgaris* 'My Favorite')

the stem until it turns brown, then plunk it into the water. This euphorbia's extravagant chartreuse blooms, which look as if they should be growing underwater rather than out in the garden, are well worth the trouble.

April 12

I cut these flowers during a cold spell when the wind was icy and the temperature barely made it into the low 40s by afternoon—still, the flowers are valiant and spring is here. Despite the continuing bone-chilling weather, the garden is blooming and leafing out enough to yield a satisfyingly large and fragrant mixed bouquet. The white and lavender lilacs in this bunch are from the neighbor's garden, traded for a bunch of freshly cut tulips.

The impetus for this bouquet was mislabeled tulips—I never meant to plant purple and white-striped ones. So I picked the interlopers out of a mass of orange tulips, figuring they wouldn't look like such a mistake in a vase. I added deep-purple, golden-centered pasqueflowers, the bartered lilacs, a few bits of just-opening, lime-green euphorbia, hot-pink spikes of bergenia flowers, and the paler, pink blooms and lacy foliage of bleeding heart, which have made it into every bouquet for a month. The lilacs add fragrance, the tulips and pasqueflowers are large enough to ground the arrangement, and the chartreuse of euphorbia and bleeding heart brighten and lighten the intensity of the darker colors. Because the striped tulips are so showy, I kept to a narrow color range that shows them off rather than competes with their vibrancy.

This slim, serrated, matte-black vase lends an edge to the early spring pastels and emphasizes the deeper, less-sweet colors in the bouquet.

White and lavender lilacs

Bleeding heart (*Dicentra spectabilis* 'Gold Heart')

Mystery tulips

Bergenia cordifolia 'Cabernet'

Euphorbia 'Blackbird'

Pasqueflower (*Pulsatilla vulgaris*)

April 21

Lilacs are all the abundance of spring in one hardy shrub, and the few, brief weeks when they bloom is a dependable marker of the season. What greater pleasure than to cut branches of white doubles, dark purples, pale lavenders (bury your nose in their delicious scent), and then bring them indoors to put by your bed, on the table where you eat breakfast, or on your desk?

Lilacs are great for trading with neighbors—why does everyone on the block need to grow the same kinds? The shrubs are large, gangly, and non-descript when out of bloom. I grow only the deep-purple, double, French

Syringa vulgaris 'My Favorite'

Various lavender and white lilacs, traded and gifted from bushes around Langley

hybrid 'My Favorite', which produces plenty of fragrant flowers. I barter those for some branches of white and lavender varieties.

Lilacs are the most versatile of flowers for arrangements—stick a single branch into a narrow vase to show off the line of the woody stem that so beautifully contrasts with the overblown beauty of the flower clusters. Add a branch of lilac to mixed bouquets for fragrance. Or jumble a big mass of colors together for a bouquet that's the essence of spring. Most often, I pile as many lilacs as I can into a square, green, glass vase. A metal vase with a bulgy base and narrow neck works well too, for it balances out the voluptuousness of the lilacs, and its subtle color and mottled surface don't detract from the absolute perfection of the flowers.

❋

April 30

When a tree peony comes into bloom (and I have only two in my garden), it's inspiration for a bouquet. Not only are the blossoms huge and brazenly beautiful, but the foliage is strikingly divided in shape and bronze in color. The flowers are so treasured by some gardeners that they protect them from rain and harsh sun with little umbrellas made for the purpose. Why not just cut one or two blossoms to bring indoors and enjoy the profound luxury of peonies up close constantly for the few weeks of the year they're in bloom?

When I saw the pale-yellow peony just opening its buds, I knew that was the centerpiece and all other aspects of the arrangement would play second fiddle to the peony's overblown beauty. This peony is a cross between a perennial peony and a tree peony, and its stems are thick, the leaves widely branching, and the flowers heavy with ruffled petals. The thick ruff of anthers in the center of the flower seem vitally alive and more like creatures than vegetative matter. You need a heavy, narrow-necked vase like this glass one to support even a single flower. I bought this spout-neck glass vase in Vancouver, B.C., years ago, and my husband still reminds me how cumbersome it was to carry home on the train. But I love how the thick glass of the vase looks almost as if it's melted and puddled out at the bottom.

The glossy, shiny sleekness and deep color of 'Queen of the Night' tulips are a perfect foil for the tissue-papery, butter-yellow of the peony. A couple of double, orange tulips droop their heavy heads over the rim of the vase and fill out the arrangement. The peony's leaves soften the transition between the distinct shapes and colors of the flowers.

If topped off regularly with cool water—vital with a narrow-necked vase—the arrangement should last five to six days and change dramatically as the peony and tulips open wide and then slowly drop their petals. It's best to set the vase on a mat so that you can let the petals fall and enjoy the bouquet in its old age as well as its youth.

✽

Paeonia (Itoh) x 'Bartzella'

Tulips 'Queen of the Night' and
'Beauty of Appledoorn'

May 8

This bouquet is for a baby shower my daughter is throwing on a Sunday morning for her dear friend, so I wanted it to look celebratory and bright to welcome Brooke's springtime baby. The flowers are overblown and romantic,

Allium aflatunense 'Purple Sensation'

Tulip 'Queen of the Night'

Clematis 'Crystal Fountain'

Geum coccineum 'Cooky'

Paeonia (Itoh) x 'Bartzella'

Bronze fennel (*Foeniculum vulgare* 'Purpureum')

Euphorbia 'Blackbird'

Spirea 'Magic Carpet'

especially the pale-yellow peony and the clematis, but the overall effect is more contemporary than English, with allium globes, bronze fennel, and euphorbia giving the bouquet a modern edge. My daughter's townhouse is simple, sleek, and modern with concrete floors and a mostly gray and white color palette, an ideal backdrop for a fluffy riot of color in a striped glass vase.

The intensely violet, spherical flower heads of ornamental onions (*Allium* spp.) anchor the bouquet; I grow dozens and dozens of allium, so I have plenty to cut. This is my last 'Queen of the Night' tulip and the end of the yellow tree peonies. A trio of lavender-blue *Clematis* 'Crystal Fountain', with their centers of frilly stamen, are nearly as showy as the tree peony. Blue hardy geraniums and bright-orange geum are the supporting players that accent the allium, peony, and clematis stars of the bouquet. The foliage of spirea, euphorbia, dark, feathery bronze fennel, and the airy golden blooms of Bowles golden sedge add texture and fill out the bouquet.

❋

May 14

There's so much going on out in the garden by mid-May that it's a question of editing rather than scavenging. For a few short weeks, we have the luxury of orchestrating colors and fragrances rather than making the best of what's at hand. I created this bouquet to show off the most glamorous clematis I grow—'Crystal Fountain', which in all its frilly, lavender beauty can look over-the-top sweet combined with other pastels.

The elegant, amber-colored raku vase helps tone down the petticoat look of the clematis, as does the brilliant-orange exbury azalea, which is also supremely fragrant. The azalea's vivid color needs to be balanced out by other strong colors, like the deep-burgundy masterwort 'Hadspen Blood',

Clematis 'Crystal Fountain'

'Gibraltar' Exbury azalea (*Rhododendron* 'Gibraltar')

Allium aflatunense 'Purple Sensation'

Coneflower (*Rudbeckia occidentalis* 'Green Wizard')

Masterwort (*Astrantia major* 'Hadspen Blood')

Euphorbia 'Blackbird'

Geum coccineum 'Cooky'

which is much prettier than its name might imply. The violet-purple *Allium* 'Purple Sensation' echoes the color of the masterwort, and its size and spherical shape offset the showy clematis, which would otherwise dominate. The spiky 'Green Wizard' coneflower is a long-lasting curiosity that, along with the green euphorbia, helps prevent such bold color contrasts from clashing.

May 20

Sometimes it takes several tries to get a bouquet the way you like it. I had this wildly patterned Mexican pitcher in mind when I went out in the garden to clip. I began with a deep-blue iris that my neighbor handed over the fence. Then I brightened it with orange geum, two kinds of euphorbia in shades of chartreuse and wine, and a lavender clematis. But the frilly clematis made the bunch look too fancy for the silly, sturdy, little vase, so I go back out to cut arugula flowers, which look as if they could be blooming alongside the road, and the little lavender balls of chive flowers.

The purple pasqueflowers that showed up in March bouquets have gone to seed, and their feathery seed heads add texture to the bunch and help lighten up the look. But it still needs something else. So I walk down the road and cut short yellow iris out of a boggy patch in a nearby pasture because I needed more yellow to match the vase creature's legs. I'll no

Blue and yellow iris

Seed heads of pasqueflower
(*Pulsatilla vulgaris*)

Euphorbia 'Blackbird'

Euphorbia dulcis 'Chameleon'

Chive blossoms

Arugula flowers

Geum coccineum 'Cooky'

doubt tinker with the bouquet several more times during its weeklong lifetime—that's why flowers from the garden are so endlessly fun and fascinating.

June 3

I never understand great big bouquets in the middle of the dining room table because they block the views and conversation of diners, rarely fit the shape of the space, and generally seem too grand for family dinners.

This trio of little gourd-like vases, with their bulging sides and neutral glaze, are small enough to run down the center of the table to show off what's happening in the garden. At this late-spring moment, on the cusp of summer, I cut a bunch of bronzy purple euphorbia 'Chameleon' to fill one of the vases with its dusky flowers. This most delicate of euphorbias tends to

Allium aflatunense 'Purple Sensation'

Spirea japonica 'Magic Carpet'

Seed heads of pasqueflower (*Pulsatilla vulgaris*)

Euphorbia dulcis 'Chameleon'

get lost in the garden, where it reads more as shadow than flower, but close up you can appreciate its light and intricate beauty. The middle vase holds a silky explosion of pasqueflower seed heads set off by the new copper foliage of 'Magic Carpet' spirea. The third vase holds a violet allium head, which when displayed solo like this shows off each tiny starburst floret.

June 10

A rare sunny day in June inspires me to ask a few friends over for lunch in the garden. Because it's so much more fun to play around with flowers than to cook, I spend the morning experimenting with different flowers and vases.

Since this is a casual al fresco lunch, I pick a mix of cottage garden–like flowers and herbs gone to seed to match the relaxed mood of the day. Lemon-yellow arugula blossoms, orange and peach wallflowers, little purple chive balls, the last of the allium, and a showy clematis gives me plenty to work with. A bit of chartreuse euphorbia softens and blends all the purples, oranges, and yellows, and a splay of icy white lacecap hydrangea, a vigorous climber that scales the fence from my neighbor's garden, adds a gauzy effect to the rest of the flowers, which are so simply shaped and colored they could have been drawn by a kid with a crayon.

The rough, simple vases, including a Japanese basket with a handle, a stoneware container with a glaze drip down the side, and little brown raku vessel, hold varying bunches of these same flowers to quite different

Arugula flowers

Orange wallflowers
(*Erysimum* 'Apricot Twist')

Peach wallflowers
(*Erysimum* 'Jenny Brook')

Clematis 'Cezanne'

Euphorbia 'Blackbird'

Allium giganteum

Epimedium leaves

effects. In the end, I group them all in the center of the table. I echo the bouquets by floating chive blossoms on the soup and garnishing the salad with arugula flowers.

SUMMER

What is closest at hand is often the hardest for us to see. At the height of summer, we slip into the hazy pleasures of fragrant bloom. The garden can seem no more than a lovely, vague, impressionistic blur, a painting of plants. The flower arranger on a mission has a great advantage here, for our eyes stay as sharp as our shears. We kneel down to cut the tiniest buds and bloom, select a uniquely gnarled branch, or pair colors and textures with containers, all of which force us to really see and appreciate the detail and potential of each plant. What might be overlooked or appear unexciting amid the great surge of summer biomass, attracts the eye when brought inside—ornamental grass plumes, branches heavy with fuzzy berries, dahlias just budding up.

Summer flower arranging is as easy as stepping outside your back door and clipping whatever is at hand or simply arranging prunings from the morning's gardening. The disadvantage of such plentitude is that summer flowers are so big and gaudy that you can end up with a vase full of stars, unsupported by character actors or bit players. When each individual blossom is distinct, they often clash with each other—think of a dinner party where each guest is a self-satisfied showboat hogging the attention. You don't want to create such a disaster at your table or in your vases.

As a general rule, avoid using roses, lilies, sunflowers, dahlias, and hydrangeas in mixed bouquets because these hefty broads of summer look best by themselves. Think of a tall, blue vase filled with golden sunflowers, a glass pitcher holding snowy 'Casablanca' lilies, or an open bowl filled with water to float a waxy, lemon-scented *Magnolia grandiflora* blossom. Nothing could be less intimidating to put together nor more evocative of summer.

And the roses! You don't need to grow classic, long-stemmed hybrid teas for cutting. A single multiheaded spray of *Rosa* 'Penelope' or 'Ballerina' is a bouquet all by itself, with roses in all stages of development from tightly curled bud to fully unfurled flower. My current favorite rose is the highly fragrant, ruffled, yellow-orange *Rosa* 'Westerland', which looks smashing arranged with the deep purple of monkshood or the glowing violet of *Verbena* 'Homestead Purple'.

Which brings us to those all-important bit players that complement the stars—the vines, foliage, and smaller flowers needed to plump up a bouquet with fluff and texture. This is what florists call "filler." When you make do with uninspiring choices like baby's breath or salal, you miss the chance to make a distinctive bouquet. This layer is as important to the bouquet, and to the garden for that matter, as the necklace on a plain black dress or the red shoes that make the outfit. It's where the artistry of flower arranging comes into play, the way you make something unique and personal out of a bunch of blooms.

Make sure you grow plenty of small flowers, some with frothy texture. Plant meadow rue (*Thalictrum*) and love-in-a-mist (*Nigella*) for their airiness, *Knautia macedonica* for its ruby buds of flowers, and lots of *Astrantia* for long-lasting, neutral-colored interest. Yarrow, diascia, snapdragons, astilbe, hardy geraniums, catmint, and ornamental grasses in both blade and bloom, provide different textures and tones to mixed bouquets. Vines look dramatic draped around and hanging down the sides of vases—little variegated ivies, akebia, small-flowered clematis, or honeysuckle belong in most arrangements.

Be sure to tuck some fragrant flowers in every bouquet—why do without the smell of summer when you have the look of it? Just a stem or two of sweet peas, heliotrope, phlox, flowering tobacco (*Nicotiana*), roses, or a single lily can permeate a room with a scent more sweetly authentic than the most expensive of aromatherapy candles.

Too often overlooked are all the magnificent foliages of summer to support and round out a bouquet. Leaves add color and contrast as well as blend and soothe disparate flower colors. Remember that you aren't stuck with the leaves on the flowers you're using; you can strip off leaves you don't like and add prettier ones, like those of shrubby, variegated dogwoods, heavenly bamboo (*Nandina*), hostas, big glossy magnolia leaves, colored smokebushes, feathery elderberry, and leathery viburnum foliage. And don't forget small trees with interesting leaves—katsura and *Cercis canadensis* 'Forest Pansy' have heart-shaped leaves in soft-green and bronzy purple, respectively.

This is the season for easy, fragrant, and leafy joys brought indoors to give us the most intense hit of summer possible in these few, short weeks.

June 21

It's a blue, blue summer solstice, and not just because June is so often wet and chilly in the Northwest. My first two crops of basil damped off, but that dismal failure is made up for by the garden blooming in glorious shades of blue and lavender, as is my neighbor's overgrown iris patch. So I decide to celebrate the colors of sea and sky with a bouquet, even though the delphinium, the star of summer blues, is waiting for a little more warmth to fully open.

The vase proves a problem. Who would have thought flowers as striking as lavender allium and midnight-blue Japanese iris wouldn't hold up to a white vase? Nope, the chalky shade bleeds the life out of these richly colored flowers. I try several more vases before settling on a plump, melon-colored vessel made by glass artist David Levi. After all, anything that holds water can be put to use as a vase, can't it?

Allium 'Globemaster'

Dutch and Japanese iris

Clematis 'Crystal Fountain' and 'Cezanne'

Geranium 'Johnson's Blue'

The shiny glass in a slightly off-kilter shape somehow suits the long-stemmed allium globes, spiky Japanese iris, and the baroque ruffles of the bearded iris. Supporting players are cobalt-colored hardy geranium and silky clematis tucked in around the base of the arrangement for visual ballast.

June 30

Finally, a blast of heat to bring on the sweet peas. Most years they're in full and fragrant bloom by my birthday in mid-June. But after such a cold spring, it was last evening before I could pick my first real bouquet of them, and their exquisite perfume, the scent of summer, fills the house.

The old-fashioned charm of sweet peas calls for the simplest of vases, like this square, green, glass pitcher that's wide at the top so as not to compress the flowers' frills. You want to give sweet peas plenty of room. Arrange a big bunch loosely in your hand, sort the colors out so that the darker shades are distributed throughout the paler blossoms. Then snip a half inch or so off the stems with a pair of sharp shears, and stick the whole bunch into a vase filled with cool water. Fluff them up, and that's all there is to dealing with such thoroughly gratifying flowers.

The time to plan your sweet pea bouquets is when you plant seeds in March. Choose the most fragrant varieties, and include a few bicolors and some of the darkest reds and purples to give dimension to your bouquets. I bought all my sweet pea seeds this year from Renee's Garden Seeds (www .reneesgarden.com), which has an impressive selection of old-fashioned kinds. Now that they're in bloom, I love particularly the dark burgundy 'Zinfandel' and the creamy pale, supremely fragrant 'April in Paris'.

Sweet peas 'Jewels of Albion' mix, 'Zinfandel', 'April in Paris', 'Cupani's Original', 'Watermelon', and 'Velvet Elegance'

July 7

Sometimes it's just too hot or hectic to compose much, so I want the easiest of bouquets to offer relief from how busy life is at the moment. I enjoy this single apricot-orange begonia floating in a blue ceramic soufflé cup as much as any bigger, more complicated bouquet. Maybe more so, for the clarity of a single flower, displayed so simply, brings a moment of blessed quiet and beauty into the day. And the begonia lasts, just like this, for a week, on my kitchen counter. I don't think I've ever appreciated this shade of blue or the color of the flower as much, before seeing the two of them alone together. Such simple arrangements show the perfection of a single summer flower.

'Fire' begonia (*Begonia* x *tuberhybrida* 'Fire')

July 15

To carry the simplicity of single-flower arrangements over to the dining room, intersperse diminutive vases with candles and run them down the middle of the table. This is most effective when nothing quite matches, but it doesn't hurt to use a long, skinny tray to gather the disparate colors and textures together. The candles light the table, and the whole look is festive yet casual, and low enough not to block conversation, although the variety

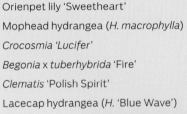

Orienpet lily 'Sweetheart'

Mophead hydrangea (*H. macrophylla*)

Crocosmia 'Lucifer'

Begonia x *tuberhybrida* 'Fire'

Clematis 'Polish Spirit'

Lacecap hydrangea (*H.* 'Blue Wave')

of blossoms might well start conversation. Refresh the water in these small vases frequently, change out flowers as they wilt, and you can keep variations of this arrangement going for weeks.

July 22

Few flowers are as easy to grow or look as elegant massed as 'Annabelle' hydrangeas. These old-fashioned flowers start out as pure-white spheres, as large as a small basketball. They mellow to a soft chartreuse as they age, and you end up with flowers in varying shades on the same shrub.

Hydrangea aborescens 'Annabelle'

I choose this tall, slender raku vase, made by Whidbey artist Al Tennant, because of its earthy look and off-white stripe that echoes the flower color. I stuff it with 'Annabelle' heads picked just before an early morning rainstorm blew in off Saratoga Passage. After the storm passed through and the garden grew steamy hot, the pale hydrangeas seemed to keep the house comfortable by radiating coolness. If harvested early in the day and conditioned in cool water, cut 'Annabelle' flowers last beautifully for a week to ten days.

❋

August 3

The scarlet spikes of *Crocosmia* 'Lucifer' and the thought of how blue hydrangeas would look in the yellow pitcher inspire this wild bouquet.

I start with the pitcher and mophead hydrangeas (*H. macrophylla*) in blue and purple. I love the play of deep blue against sunny yellow and the contrast of the shiny pitcher and matte hydrangeas. My son gave me the sunny Le Creuset pitcher for my birthday, and I have been waiting impatiently for the hydrangeas to color so I could pair them up.

I add a few lilies in flower and in bud, and tuck a couple of 'Roguchi' clematis in at the bottom where their purple bell-shaped flowers could drape the sides of the pitcher and balance out the melodrama of the flaming crocosmia.

When I step back, it seems that every element is trying to dominate. So I go back out to the garden, searching for more subtle flowers. I snip a half-dozen *Rudbeckia* 'Green Wizard', and add them as supporting players to tone it all down a bit. Still, the vigor of the bouquet surprises me—even with the rudbeckia, the overall effect is one of bursting motion.

Crocosmia 'Lucifer'

Clematis 'Roguchi'

Rudbeckia 'Green Wizard'

Orienpet lily 'Sweetheart'

Hydrangea macrophylla 'Altona'

August 11

I cut a few late lilies and brought them inside to prolong their beauty and perfume as long as possible. I just can't believe another lily season is past. I'd resolved not to plant any more this fall because my little garden is overwhelmed with lily blossom and scent in late July and early August—yet

Oriental lilies
Clematis 'Polish Spirit'

I'm already plotting where just a few more bulbs can be squeezed into the ground in November.

It's a good idea to keep the vase simple when dealing with such extravagant flowers. This amber-colored cylinder is plain enough in shape yet strong enough in color to work with lilies. I put these lilies together for an opening night at Museo Gallery in Langley, so it's photographed in an all-white setting that suits the showy lilies.

It's difficult to mix lilies with other flowers because smaller blossoms are diminished by the blatant boldness of lilies. I try tucking a few snowy 'Annabelle' hydrangeas in here, but it looks like a couple of prima donnas duking it out. Yet one single kind of lily seems insufficient, so I stick in several kinds of different sizes, with some purple clematis tumbling down the side of the vase for a contrast in texture and shape. The deep, velvety color of the clematis shows off the lily's luminescent silkiness, and the vine's lax drape balances out the stiff uprightness of the lily stems.

❋

August 17

This little bouquet of humble flowers, mostly sneezeweed and honeysuckle, is sweet and intimate, perfect to put by a guest's bedside or on a side table to sniff as you pass by. The colors are richly ripe, redolent of summer at its peak.

Sneezeweed (*Helenium autumnale*)

Sweet peas

Honeysuckle (*Lonicera* x *heckrottii* 'Goldflame')

Crocosmia 'Solfatare'

The dog days of August can be hard on flowers, even tough, old-fashioned ones like these. Be sure to pick early in the morning on hot days, when flowers are freshest and still refreshed by overnight dew.

The purple sweet peas, as well as the honeysuckle, are strongly fragrant and fill in around the apricot-golden crocosmia that's just come into bloom. This small-scale variety, called 'Solfatare', has spiky, bronze foliage that not only complements the flower color to perfection, but adds drama to any arrangement. Sneezeweed, in all the quintessential golds and rusts of late summer, is the star of the bouquet. These willowy perennials can be hazardous to cut because of all the busy honeybees that flock to it. Sneezeweed is my favorite of all the daisylike flowers because it lasts a long time in the garden and in the vase, and I love its warm, brown centers that remind me of a dog's soft nose. The vase is clear orange glass, small and slim, so as not to distract from the perfection of the most simple summer flowers.

❋

August 25

How can it already be time for harvest bouquets? Despite the autumnal plant palette, I try to keep this bouquet summery looking with some fat sunflowers to balance out the extravagant dahlia, the biggest, showiest one I grew all summer. The buff and green jug is heavy and round enough to suit this heavy-headed bouquet, and it holds enough water to keep it fresh.

With a flower as full of bravado as the bicolored cactus dahlia, a bouquet needs plenty of fluffing out with flowers that are distinct in their own right. Here spiky golden crocosmia plays off all the round dahlias and sneezeweed, and the colors and shapes are reinforced by a double-echo effect. The orange and golden stripes of the sneezeweed mirror the dahlia, and their brown centers in turn are magnified by the sunflowers' wide, chocolate centers. This deep color is repeated in some of the hypericum berries that are beginning to turn their darker fall color.

Hypericum androsaemum 'Albury Purple'

Cactus dahlia (no idea what kind—it was a gift from a friend's garden)

Sunflowers (*Helianthus annuus*)

Crocosmia 'Solfatare'

Sneezeweed (*Helenium autumnale*)

September 10

Only a week after a fat yellow and red ruffled dahlia anchored a summer bouquet, it feels as though autumn has descended. That same dahlia looks very different in an autumnal arrangement. A ribbed wooden cylinder of a vase (with a glass inside to hold water) in a dark bordeaux color emphasizes that even though October isn't here yet, the garden looks as though it is.

The hot-orange single dahlia is 'Forncett Furnace', an old, vigorous variety that blooms like crazy and lasts well after it's cut. A couple of mophead hydrangeas tucked in around the bottom of the bouquet cool down the hot-colored flowers and ground the bouquet with their globular shape. Yarrow, with its flat heads of tiny flowers, lightens the look with its paler color and finer texture; deep-purple *Sedum* 'Black Jack' adds sculptural shadows. Peruvian lilies and dependable golden sneezeweed fill out the bouquet. The cinnamon-colored, droopy spikes of love-lies-bleeding finishes off the bunch with its weird look of soft, chenille fingers poking up through the blossoms.

Simply snip a decent length of stem (cut to a pair of next year's developing buds), strip off the lower leaves or even all the leaves, and stick the hydrangeas into a roomy vase (don't crowd them) with a couple of inches of water in the bottom. The water slowly evaporates, leaving the hydrangeas beautifully dried for fall or even holiday arrangements.

Yarrow (*Achillea millefolium* 'Terra Cotta')

Love-lies-bleeding (*Amaranthus cruentus* 'Hot Biscuit')

Sedum 'Black Jack'

Dahlia 'Forncett Furnace'

Hydrangea macrophylla

Peruvian lily (*Alstroemeria* 'Butterscotch')

Sneezeweed (*Helenium autumnale*)

AUTUMN

It's not that I didn't appreciate every single hellebore and daffodil that bloomed during the cold, wet spring. I swooned when a heat wave brought forth a burst of lilies. I've been thankful to harvest tomatoes and sweet peas since July. But now, during the garden's waning weeks, I relax into its pleasures and see every flower, falling leaf, and pumpkin most clearly.

By autumn, the garden is what it is. Nothing is more precious than picking one of the last roses of the season; nothing sweeter than popping a final raspberry into your mouth. The tiny, emerald-green frogs are singing in the

garden, and there's a new black lamb in the pasture on a warm September morning in Langley. The sun slants through the thick mist, a perfect day to harvest hydrangeas. Now's the time to gather mopheads to dry—the whole trick is in the timing. Picked too soon, the petals shrivel up. You want to wait until the flower heads turn a little leathery right on the bush. By that time, the blossoms will already be changing from blue and purple to vintage wallpaper shades of faded mauve, green, and plum.

Simply snip a decent length of stem (cut to a pair of next year's developing buds), strip off the lower leaves or even all the leaves, and stick the hydrangeas into a roomy vase (don't crowd them) with a couple of inches of water in the bottom. The water slowly evaporates, leaving the hydrangeas beautifully dried for fall or even holiday arrangements.

Hydrangea macrophylla

Luxuriant summer bouquets start to look all wrong once the mornings become chilly enough to see your breath. Autumn is a time to come indoors and enjoy the pleasures of the fireplace, warm lamplight, and hot soup. The maturing colors of autumn foliage and flowers add to this atmosphere of drawing in.

The burnished, slightly faded, autumn colors all go together so harmoniously that there's no need to worry about matches or clashes. Think of the soft mauves of dried hydrangea heads, the wheat and creamy white of ornamental grass fluorescences, the rich purple-bronze of smokebush (*Cotinus* spp.) foliage. Combined and brought indoors, they glow softly, almost as if their leaves and blossoms carry the scent of wood smoke and crunchy apples. Add the surprise of a few fat rugosa rose hips and a branch of those renegade blackberries that poke through the fence, letting the berries drip down the side of the vase. You've created the essence of autumn in a vase.

Now in the weaker autumn sunlight, I love weedy arrangements that look as if I've spent a day in the country, gathering whatever was at hand. Rough stoneware vases or glazed pitchers in soft shades of blue, olive, and caramel look great stuffed full of sunflowers, coneflowers, rudbeckia, the last dahlias, leaves, and the feathery blooms of ornamental grasses. It can be just that easy in autumn.

Though a few remaining roses, nasturtiums, and hardy geraniums are still out there, I pass them by for the subtler autumn beauty of hydrangea heads (kissed by frost into deep shades of plum and mossy green), ferns, and other foliage plants that come into their own now. Go for contrast—the glossy leaves of sasanqua camellia shine when paired with golden yew or dark, ruffled kale. Once a serious freeze hits the garden, usually in mid-November in my zone 8 garden, there won't even be many of these choices.

In autumn, you can still cut whole branches of Japanese maple, sourwood (*Oxydendrum arboreum*) with its brilliant scarlet leaves, or flame-red burning bush (*Euonymus alata*) to stick in a basket on the hearth (lined with a water-filled jar). The berry-laden branches of hawthorns, pyracantha, and crab apples provide line, color, and fruit. For a more traditional bouquet, dahlias, asters, or chrysanthemums look lovely with maroon Virginia creeper vines or with bunches of herbs clipped just before the first frost hits. Although summer can still linger into October, soon after Halloween autumn has had its way with our gardens. The season's downward momentum is in full swing. We may as well enjoy what's left for as long as we can.

※

October 1

This single blossom of matilija poppy, which really isn't a poppy at all, deserves its own vase. I set it on the windowsill, where the afternoon sun shines through its crinkled petals and shows off their tissue-paper texture. Also known as the egg yolk plant for its explosion of yellow stamen, it blooms long and late, growing wild as a weed in warmer climates. Yet it's supremely beautiful when singled out and treated like the little piece of exotica that it is.

Matilija poppy (*Romneya coulteri*)

The smooth, shiny, metal vase with its tiny frogs is a treasure I found more than 30 years ago at Gump's in San Francisco. I have used it often since because its narrow throat is perfect for displaying a single stem.

October 15

Picking the last really big, fill-your-arms bouquet in autumn is a bitter-sweet pleasure. Still, it should probably be acknowledged as a seasonal marker, if not celebrated as joyously as the first big bouquet in spring. Although I still have sweet little raspberries, increasingly skimpy dahlias, and nasturtiums that are acting as if it's still midsummer, the garden is mostly winding down, and I feel almost as if I am stripping it clean to make this bouquet.

I have to fight my way past the spiderwebs to harvest these final dahlias, Northern sea oats, sneezeweed, an artichoke past its prime, hydrangea, and grape-colored penstemon that is reblooming accommodatingly late in the season. I've been away from the garden except for brief watering drive-bys, for weeks, traveling and then busy in the city. In my absence, the spiders took over, wrapping shrubs and perennials in their sticky, dewy master-pieces. If spiders are the sign of a healthy garden, mine is doing great. The dahlias had a boost from a week of warm weather, as did the sneezeweed. The red 'Forncett Furnace' dahlia is still going strong, and their yellow cen-ters inspire the choice of vase. The green tomatoes tell the story of a chilly summer followed by fall arriving a couple of weeks too soon (doesn't it always?) and the grape leaves turned burning red play off the intense color of the dahlias.

Dahlias and hydrangeas

Northern sea oats (*Chasmanthium latifolium*)

Purple-leaf ornamental grape (*Vitis vinifera* 'Purpurea')

Italian purple artichoke

Green tomatoes

Sneezeweed (*Helenium autumnale*)

Curly purple kale

I wish for a few sprays of purple and watermelon-colored asters for color contrast. As I put this bouquet together, I resolve to shoehorn in at least one hot-pink 'Alma Poetschke' aster, and a plant or two of the long blooming, purple-blue *Aster* x *frikartii* 'Monch' to add to next year's final, bounteous bouquet.

October 22

A burst of spiky green blades striped in horizontal bands of gold, zebra grass is as pretty in the vase as it is in the garden. The pickings are getting slim out there as the rains set in, but ornamental grasses are looking their best this time of year. Count on their strong foliage and fluffy flowers to carry late season bouquets.

Miscanthus sinensis 'Little Zebra'

Hydrangea macrophylla

Curly purple kale

Coral bark maple (*Acer palmatum* 'Sango-kaku')

'Little Zebra' is a dwarf version of miscanthus, perfect for smaller gardens because it tops out at 2 to 3 feet high. The foliage is stiff and fanlike, which is why it stands up so well to autumn rain and wind. But it also means you need to mix this sternly upright grass with rounded flower shapes and foliage to avoid a rigid, military effect. Here, zebra grass adds height to a bouquet softened out by a mauvey-blue head of mophead hydrangea, frilly purple kale, and a spray of coral bark maple leaves chosen for their finely textured foliage already turned bright yellow. I think the reason this simple bouquet, composed of just four elements, works is that the vase is handmade (by Whidbey artist Al Tennant) and interesting all by itself. Then each part of the bouquet is distinctive and different; the grass is striped and spiky, the kale is dark and frilly, the hydrangea is distinctly spherical, and the Japanese maple leaves, with their finer texture and windblown look, lighten and brighten the composition.

You can leave this bouquet to dry, and it lasts for more than a week, especially if you don't mind the maple leaves drifting down and piling up around the base of the vase.

✻

November 1

A Pineapple express blows through today with drenching rains, so I run out to rescue a few, last Japanese maple branches for a Day of the Dead bouquet. The leaves have turned such saturated gold that all you need is a simple, dark vase with a strong, solid look to play off the twiggyness of the maple branches and the ephemeral look of their ethereal golden leaves.

Japanese maple leaves

If you smash the bottom of the branches, or roughly cut them at an angle so they suck up water, the branches hold on to their leaves for several days. Arrange the branches as three-dimensionally as possible in plenty of cool water. No matter how tenderly you treat them, the branches drop their leaves soon enough, so set the vase on a mat that won't be stained by the falling foliage. The bouquet will change throughout the week, with the structure of the branches revealed as the leaves drift down, echoing what's going on outside right now.

✳

November 9

The dark wooden vase is richly warm in color and texture, perfect for the chocolate silk tree, also known as purple-leaf mimosa, which is the focal point in this big, messy bouquet. This little tree remains stubbornly sticklike through June, its leaves coming on frustratingly late in spring. But it makes up for it at the tail end of the season, hanging on to its dramatic foliage much later than most other trees. The soft-green berries are from an Oregon grape stripped of its toothed leaves to show off the fruit. Autumn ferns fluff out the bunch, along with grasses, rose hips, and glossy camellia leaves.

These materials aren't very cooperative because they're stiff, scratchy, and sometimes so fragile by this late in the season, especially the pennisetum blooms, that they seem to dissolve in your hand. This unruliness is

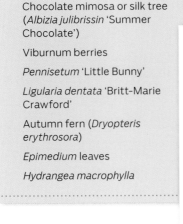

Chocolate mimosa or silk tree (*Albizia julibrissin* 'Summer Chocolate')

Viburnum berries

Pennisetum 'Little Bunny'

Ligularia dentata 'Britt-Marie Crawford'

Autumn fern (*Dryopteris erythrosora*)

Epimedium leaves

Hydrangea macrophylla

part of their charm because they bring a sense of nature to the vase in a way more perfect flowers never can. Right now, when they're dying down for the winter, is when we need our gardens most. It's a relief to get the feel of them right in the middle of the dining-room table. I swear this bouquet even smells fresh and cold like the weather. Is flower arranging folk art? If the definition of folk art is genuine emotion shared with others, then maybe it is.

November 20—Thanksgiving Week

Three little Japanese bowls are perfect vessels to hold a loose assortment of textural twigs, leaves, berries, and pods. Using a number of small elements like these on a holiday table makes it simple to arrange and rearrange, depending on how many people and serving bowls you need room for.

Ligularia dentata 'Britt-Marie Crawford' seedpods

Viburnum berries

Senecio greyi 'Sunshine'

Hebe 'Amy'

Granny's ringlets Japanese cedar (*Cryptomeria japonica* 'Spiralis')

Columnar Irish yew (*Taxus baccata* 'Fastigiata')

Key to making such a diversity of pickings look harmonious rather than random is repeating elements in each bowl. Curly kale, rose hips, viburnum berries, and conifer clippings make an appearance in each bowl, but the ligularia seedpods, silvery senecio, and glossy purple hebe are used in only one bowl each, making the bowls distinctive.

The colors (not that I had much to choose from out there) were inspired by the muted floral table runner I always pull out in late fall. Because holiday decorations tend to be grand and sparkly, I particularly love this simple, natural approach, which lets the food, conversation, and candlelight star.

Don't worry about slug nibbles in the epimedium or a slight shred on the kale leaves—such imperfections suit the nature of these humble bouquets and speak of nature and the garden, which we welcome this dark time of year when we stay indoors so much of the time.

✤

November 27

I love how this tangle of rose hips brings a familiar painting alive and makes me see the art with fresh eyes. The painting is by Whidbey Island artist Marianne Brabanski, and the rose hips are from an old climbing rose in my neighbor's garden. The vase is tall, cylindrical, green glass, and I just stuck as many rose branches in there as I could. The smoky elegance of the

The fruit from an unknown variety of old climbing rose

vase plays off the wild nature of the unassuming rose hips. The big, fat fruit on rugosa roses makes stunning bouquets too, but you don't have such long canes to work with.

✳

December 5

The same vase, same scene, this time with the boughs and fuzzy buds of deciduous magnolias. This arrangement dries and lasts for many weeks. Or if you keep a few inches of fresh water in the vase, the buds slowly crack open, even though they've been cut far too soon to force into bloom. That's okay—the plump, creaturelike, furry buds are striking in and of themselves; the way they curve and twist in the vase is an extra pleasure.

Buds of Magnolia 'Elizabeth'

December 18

It's time for a simplicity break. Quiet winter beauty is so welcome amid the rush and glitz of the holidays. Majestic magnolia leaves make a bouquet all by themselves, loosely arranged in a raku vase. This is *Magnolia grandiflora*

Magnolia grandiflora 'Victoria'

'Victoria'—a small evergreen tree that's perfectly hardy to USDA zone 7, despite its Southern, warm-weather good looks. The bud hints of the large, fragrant, ivory flowers that open in summer. But for now, the magnolia's glossy green leaves, in contrast to their furry golden-brown undersides (called *indementum*, an attribute with which some species of magnolia are more blessed than others) are understated perfection.

I love that you need to cut only a few branches to have a stunning arrangement that lasts for a couple of weeks, even in a warm room. The only other winter shrub or tree that I can think of that makes an arrangement all by itself is the strawberry tree (*Arbutus unedo*), with handsome bark, little white flowers, narrow evergreen leaves, and bumpy little red fruits (hence the common name) all happening at the same time in early winter. But for now, I'm content with the elegance and simplicity of magnolia leaves.

WINTER

Winter arrangements are like vegetarian cooking—just as there's no slab of meat to plunk down in the middle of the plate as the centerpiece of the meal, there aren't any bravado lilies, roses, or delphinium to build an arrangement around. Winter bouquets are bits and pieces of what remains during the darkest, coldest days, often picked close to the ground, foraged from alleys, or traded with friends and neighbors. Not everyone has room for a holly tree in the garden.

It's worth it to get out on a cold morning and pick, not only to stay connected with nature and your garden in a season when we're most often sheltering indoors, but also so you have an alternative to store-bought tulips in the house, which whisper about nothing other than hothouses and truck transport. Even the most modest twigs of red dogwood or pine needles remind us of deep winter and nature's architectural beauty.

The gathering isn't as easy now though, because you can't just run outside in flip-flops and find more to cut than you imagined. You need to use different eyes when you're scavenging the garden for cuttings this time of year, while encumbered by boots, woolly hat, and warm gloves. Look high and low, for ground-hugging plants are as vital to a lively bouquet as tree branches this time of year. Purple euphorbia tips, frost-burnished epimedium, and bits and pieces of daphnes and hebes add texture and color to the mostly evergreen palette. Think more about texture, berries, and pods than about flower or color, and be glad you have thick gloves on when you go after the prickly, deeply toothed leaves of Oregon grape or bristly conifer boughs.

Vases play a key role in winter arrangements because now we need to rely on the strength of their colors, finishes, and shapes as we never do during the garden's more bountiful months. Metallic vases add gloss to all the materials that don't have much luster themselves. A vase's patina can be used to balance out the bristle of pine needles, the roughness of conifers.

And fragrance? Grow a rosemary shrub or two for the clean, spicy scent of its foliage, and plant sarcococca for its supremely sweet-smelling white flowers in the dead of winter.

In winter, when our plants may look a little ragged and scraggly, is a good time to get over perfectionism. I don't wear my reading glasses, let alone bifocals, when arranging. A little softness around the edges is good because it blurs our too-critical eye and helps us see our arrangements as others will see them. Think of the famous English designer Gertrude

Jekyll, who designed all those gorgeous impressionistic borders as she was going blind. She wasn't able to see details anymore, so she reveled in blocks of color, sweeps of texture, form and shape, which is just what you need to do with winter arrangements, on a much smaller scale.

The garden is resilient and persistent. Soon enough and ever so slowly, the days will lengthen, the garden will come alive, and we'll welcome every single daffodil and hellebore as if they were the roses of summer.

❀

New Year's Day Bouquets

It's 25 degrees and seriously frosty in Langley, but the sun is out, and so am I, clippers in hand to scavenge what I can after nearly a week of freezing temperatures. It's down to the basics out there. Nothing jumps out at me; the garden is almost bare and wintry brown, but I'm looking for a bit of texture and any bright foliage I can find.

In the absence of flowers, the trick is to play contrasting textures and shades against one other. I cut bits of conifer, clusters of stiff, skinny pine needles, and heart-shaped epimedium leaves turned red by the cold. What these earthy materials lack in variety of color is made up by their quiet redolence of nature.

I recruited three shiny, mottled candleholders as vases, relieved that they all seem to hold water. Two hold a single kind of plant to make the greatest impact. Granny's ringlets is a dwarf conifer that stays small enough

Granny's ringlets Japanese cedar (*Cryptomeria japonica* 'Spiralis')

Weeping white pine (*Pinus strobus* 'Pendula')

Epimedium

Dwarf Monterey cypress (*Cupressus macrocarpa* 'Wilma Goldcrest')

Rosemary

to fit into even the tiniest urban garden; and the dense, swirled foliage stays bright chartreuse through the winter. Another vase holds a bristled splay of blue-green pine; the third is a mixed bunch of pine, epimedium, rosemary, and chartreuse Monterey cypress. The rosemary releases its herby scent in the warm room, and the epimedium lends its heart-shaped, red-tinted leaves to play off the narrow needles and warm green of the conifers.

❋

January 8

I decide to photograph this bouquet outside so you can see that the garden yields clippings and even flowers even when there's a dusting of snow. Can't believe that this Corsican hellebore cultivar is budded and even blooming—it's planted beneath a hydrangea and so has some shelter from the cold wind. 'Silver Lace' is one of the earliest blooming hellebores, with jagged silvery leaves and soft green blossoms centered in chartreuse stamen. Evergreen huckleberry leaves, turned to shades of plum, pink, and purple by the cold, pick up the color in the bright twigs of coral bark maple.

When dealing with thick, congested evergreens, plants damaged by cold, or a hellebore like this one, the leaves of which dominate the flower, just get out your clippers and snip and shape away. Branches are often too heavy for a vase—or anyway, they *look* too dense and heavy. Use sharp clippers to thin them out and shape them as you like—in this bouquet only the pine had a shape elegant enough to avoid the clippers.

I stripped off all the big hellebore leaves, leaving two or three small ones because their silvery sheen played off the vase's finish. I filled in with

Helleborus argutifolius 'Silver Lace'

Evergreen huckleberry (*Vaccinium ovatum*)

Coral bark maple twigs

Weeping white pine (*Pinus strobus* 'Pendula')

the huckleberries, whose airy texture and red-tinged leaves show off the pale hellebore flowers. I chose a tall, sturdy pewter vase to hold the bouquet securely; its patina seemed to reflect the snow.

✳

January 25

I've had this squat little bronze vase for years, and I pull it out every winter to spice up simple arrangements. The vase's warm gloss shows off the red leaves of the epimedium, burnished by frost, with their wiry stems and green veins. The heart-shaped leaves contrast with the stiff, skinny needles of the pine. I've tucked in rosemary for fragrance, and the Granny's ringlets for texture.

Epimedium

Weeping white pine (*Pinus strobus* 'Pendula')

Granny's ringlets Japanese cedar (*Cryptomeria japonica* 'Spiralis')

February 2

Not much more than witch hazel is in bloom out there these dark days, but it's surprising how much mileage you can get from its peculiar little fragrant flowers and stiff branches. Really, witch hazel is better in a vase than in the ground because out in the landscape the blossoms can almost disappear; all you see is the gangly vase-shape of the shrub itself. Indoors, close up, the flowers are intriguing, with their spidery filaments and sweetly clean, astringent scent.

Hamamelis x *intermedia* 'Jelena'

Although a modern metallic vase might seem an odd choice to hold such rustic-looking branches, I like how its slim, shiny sweep glams up the matte of the bark and dark flowers. The metal's silver sheen shows off the copper color of the *Hamamelis* x *intermedia* 'Jelena' flowers. These darker witch hazels aren't as cheery in the garden as the more common yellow bloomers, but at close range, their flower color is striking. The bottle is by Kirkland artist Deloss Webber.

❋

February 14

Such a temptation to buy some of the cut flowers on sale for Valentine's Day—made easier to resist by the ridiculous prices and the fact red flowers are way down my list. But still, I must be influenced by the showiness of the big bunches (or perhaps I'm just tired of winter), because I group a pot of little narcissus (yes, bought at the grocery store, but on its way to be planted in the garden) with the starlike, fragrant flowers of *Clematis armandii* and pussy willows in a melon-colored glass vase for ballast and backdrop.

The little raku vase, with its squat shape and coarse, dark finish, plays up the delicate beauty of the star-shaped, sweetly fragrant clematis. This vine has evergreen leaves, and it blooms for a full month, starting in mid-February, depending on the weather. You can see the buds are just opening, and the scent is heavenly. The pussy willows are at their plump and furry best right now. Nothing means spring like narcissus, and these tiny ones

Pussy willows

Clematis montana

Dwarf narcissus

are faintly fragrant and cheerily bright. You could swap out smaller vases and pots for weeks to freshen up the arrangement, and the pussy willows dry beautifully if you don't put any water in the vase.

February 28

The weather feels like we're on the cusp of spring, warm enough to open the tiny, fragrant flowers of winter daphne. The hybrid hellebores have been blooming for a couple of weeks now, and this purple one shows up better in the vase than in the garden. To keep hellebores looking fresh after cutting,

Winter daphne (*Daphne odora* 'Marginata')

Helleborus x *hybridus*

Euphorbia 'Red Martin' and 'Blackbird'

slice the stem up a few inches before putting them in a vase, so they can drink plenty of water. And even though it's painful to do, I try to cut a couple of stems with buds. I'm not sure why, but hellebores are especially pleasing to watch as they open. Maybe it's just because they're the most satisfyingly large and exquisite flowers we can grow this time of year.

A paler, freckled hellebore and two kinds of euphorbia (one purple, the other blue-green) round out the bouquet, along with the daphne for perfume. I use this amber vase pretty much year-round for its cylindrical shape and mottled finish that reminds me of tree bark. It seems to complement every color of foliage and flower, except maybe pink or red, which I grow so little of that it doesn't matter.

March 14

Warm Chinook winds blow the scent of spring through the garden, the little bulbs are up and blooming, and the trees are acquiring an encouraging haze of fresh green that'll pop out into leaves in a few weeks.

The orange and green vase is "Carrot Top" by Whidbey Island artist Johanna Marquis. The grouping of multistemmed, narrow vases is perfect for displaying tiny spring beauties like these earliest narcissus, crocus, and plum blossoms. For contrast, I added a backdrop of the silvery-white pods of the money penny plant, a biennial that is a weedy nuisance, really. I picked the pods last autumn from an alley behind my house, where they

Money penny or honesty
(*Lunaria biennis*)

Miniature narcissus (from a
fragrant seedling mix)

Crocus vernus 'Remembrance'

Plum blossoms

grow and spread about in a big, wild patch. They kept all winter in this
tall raku vase, a contrast in their papery winter look to the bright colors of
near-springtime.

Lilies, nasturtium, alstroemeria and dahlias growing in feed troughs and raised beds .

what to grow:
a core list

What you grow in your garden depends on the climate where you live, your topography, taste, time, and size of garden. Because just about any plant has potential for bouquets, there's a whole big world out there of possibilities.

This lists forms a core collection of plants that yield flowers, leaves, boughs, colored stems, seed heads, or dried flowers in every month of the year—again, depending on the climate in which you garden. Every one of these plants is a dependable multitasker, as useful in the garden as cut for the vase. Some, like artichokes, cardoons, and rainbow chard are delicious to eat as well. The happy fact is that plants that do best in the garden are usually star performers in the vase as well.

Follow nature's cue and plant in layers, so you can cut from the ground up to the trees. Always go for flowers with character; every poppy, rose, and lily has its own unique shape, as opposed to carnations or marigolds that look pretty much all the same. When you cut a single flower for your desk, you want individuality, not bland uniformity.

Don't forget herbs, fruits, and vegetables such as rosemary, chive, and arugula flowers or cherry tomatoes and raspberry canes heavy with berries; they add color, texture, fragrance, and surprise to bouquets. You can cut from your garden and eat it too.

Leaves last longer than flowers, so plant plenty of foliage plants that appeal to you. Find out which evergreen shrubs are dependably hardy in your climate, and plant a few to carry your garden and vases through the seasons. Leaf texture (pleated, ribbed, feathery), variegation, size, and shape keep your garden and arrangements interesting through the year.

Simply think of planting a succession of living, growing choices, a parade of leaf, flower, berry, branch, and pod. Your garden continually evolves, which will in turn keep your bouquets lively and engaging.

Most important, pay attention to your own heart and eye. Give garden room to only the plants you love best. Revel in color, swoon over fragrances that stir your associations and memories. Even though mock orange is a big, gangly plant, I've always managed to squeeze one into any garden I've made. When it blooms in June, its supremely sweet scent is a satisfaction not to be bought at any price. I still marvel that such luxuries are easy to grow in your own backyard. Witch hazel's spidery little flowers in the dead of winter, statuesque May alliums, and armfuls of fragrant sweet peas offer that same sense of luxury through the seasons. Have fun finding your own touchstone plants.

If you think of growing a garden as one big, marvelous, creative experiment, you'll grow right along with your garden. As long as you take care matching plants to conditions (right plant, right place), and consider eventual size and spread, you'll love your garden, and it will yield a gratifying supply of bouquet fodder.

All the plants in these lists are hardy to at least USDA zone 7; many are much hardier. None are finicky or tricky to grow if you give them good soil, adequate water, and the amount of sunshine they require—all information that's easy to find online or in any basic gardening book written for your climate.

You'll see many of the plants in these lists used over and over again in the bouquets in this book. They're the backbone of my garden. Others are plants I long to have room for—maybe in my next garden. In the meantime, I hope my neighbors grow them so I can trade, or I make do with the next best thing, which gardens are extraordinarily generous in providing.

SPRING

Snowdrops, crocus, and daffodils flower early, like the small, fragrant Pheasant's eye (*Narcissus poeticus* var. *recurvus*) or the amber 'Serola'.

Tulips bloom a little later in spring, and although they're readily available in flower markets, you have a much greater choice if you grow them yourself. Favorites include the ruffly pink 'Angelique', silky dark 'Queen of the Night', and the vivid-orange 'Beauty of Appledoorn'.

Clematis armandii is a vigorous evergreen vine with fragrant, white flowers in March.

French lilacs (*Syringa vulgaris*) are tall shrubs with fragrant spring flowers from white to dark purple.

Korean spice viburnum (*V. carlesii*) is a handsome deciduous shrub with large (for a viburnum) pink flowers that bloom for a month in early spring and smell like cloves.

Allium are bulbs in the onion family that bloom May into June. The tall purple ones like 'Globemaster', 'Giganteum', and 'Purple Sensation' are gorgeous in the ground and the vase. Star of Persia (*Allium christophii*) is shorter stemmed with a starry lavender head the size of a small basketball.

Bleeding heart (*Dicentra spectabilis*) is a perennial that produces more and more finely dissected leaves and pink flowers the more you cut it. 'Gold Heart' is a slap of chartreuse leaves intensified by hot-pink valentine flowers.

Peonies have handsome foliage that turns shades of red in autumn; the new Itoh hybrids have especially gorgeous big, ruffled flowers in May. Favorites are the warm yellow 'Bartzella' and the uniquely colored 'Kopper Kettle'.

SUMMER

Dahlias are old-fashioned showboats that anchor bouquets summer into autumn. Look for single ones like the orange 'Fornett's Furnace' and purple-foliaged 'Clarion' and 'Dark Angel' series because they work well in concert with other plants in the garden and are showy cut for bouquets.

Lavender (*Lavandula* spp.) plants are sub-shrubs with pretty gray-green foliage and wands of fragrant flowers that can scent every summer bouquet; they also dry easily.

Lilies are stars in the garden and the vase. From the classic, huge, white 'Casablanca' to the new Orienpets, you can't go wrong if you choose fragrant varieties. Lilies take up little space in the garden. If you plant for succession, you can have lilies in bloom from June through September.

Honeysuckle (*Lonicera* spp.) are easy, tough vines with bright, fragrant flowers. Favorites include *Lonicera* x *heckrottii* 'Goldflame' and the creamy, highly scented *Lonicera periclymenum* 'Graham Thomas'.

Sweet peas (*Lathyrus odoratus*) grow easily from seed and are supremely fragrant and ruffled, an ideal cut flower. Some of the most sweetly scented and beautifully colored include 'Zinfandel', 'April in Paris', 'Velvet Elegance', and 'Watermelon'.

Clematis vary from wide, spreading flowers to tiny bell-shaped blooms, followed by fluffy seed heads; grow all of these vines that you can find space for. The new Polish cultivars are especially long lasting, easy to grow, and deeply colored.

Wallflowers (*Erysimum cheiri*) bloom all summer with cheery, fragrant, little flowers.

Peruvian lilies (*Alstroemeria* spp.) have stamina; no perennial flower lasts longer when cut. The more unusual peach or blush-colored types such as 'Butterscotch' aren't as invasive as the common orange ones.

Hydrangeas, whether mopheads or paniculata, lack for nothing but fragrance. These showy flowers dry beautifully and last all winter indoors. Favorites include *H. serrata* 'Preziosa', *H. aborescens* 'Annabelle' (left), and the oakleaf *H. quercifolia* 'Snowflake'.

Roses impose a little homework on gardeners. Figure out which kind do best in your climate, and go for fragrance. English roses, or David Austin roses, have the fragrance and frilly beauty of old-fashioned roses but bloom much longer. Favorites include *Rosa* 'Penelope', 'Iceberg', the species rose *R. mutabilis*, 'Ballerina', and 'Westerland'.

Also for summer into autumn, try geum, crocosmia, hardy geraniums, yarrow, poppies, coneflowers, sea holly, sedum, sunflowers, bee balm, nasturtiums, astrantia, kniphofia, and rudbeckia.

AUTUMN

Hardy fuchsias bloom until frost; *F. magellanica* 'Aurea' has golden foliage with pink and purple flowers.

Sneezeweed (*Helenium autumnale*) is a tall perennial with daisylike flowers, centered with brown almost like (very) mini-sunflowers. It starts blooming in summer and continues nearly until frost.

Autumn fern (*Dryopteris erythrosora*) has two-foot-tall, russet-toned, evergreen fronds.

Purple grape vine (*Vitis vinifera* 'Purpurea') has handsome purple foliage all summer and turns a luminous deep red in autumn.

Sedum 'Autumn Joy' and 'Jack Black' are two of the taller sedums to fill out autumn bouquets.

Aster x *frikartii* 'Mönch' is the longest-blooming aster, with blue-toned flowers centered in yellow.

Ornamental-grass blooms give a casual, wildflower look to autumn bouquets, especially miscanthus such as 'Little Zebra' with striped foliage, all the pennisetums with brush-like flowers, and Northern sea oats (*Chasmanthium latifolium*) with drooping, faintly reptilian blooms.

Camellia sasanqua are lax, evergreen shrubs ideal to espalier for their glossy deep-green leaves and ruffled flowers that bloom off and on through winter. *C. sasanqua* 'Setsugekka' has huge double white flowers that begin blooming in October.

WINTER

Mahonia x *media* 'Charity' is a tall Oregon grape with jagged foliage and fragrant yellow flowers in January. *Mahonia nervosa* is a much shorter type; all are evergreen with pretty berries.

Red-barked dogwood (*Cornus alba*) and coral bark maple (*Acer palmatum* 'Sango-kaku') are good choices for bright-pink and red winter branches and twigs.

Arbutus unedo has evergreen leaves, handsome bark, and in winter, white flowers and bright red fruits.

Viburnum davidii is a tough, low-growing shrub with pleated, leathery evergreen leaves and brilliant blue berries.

Viburnum tinus is a larger evergreen shrub with clusters of fragrant white flowers all winter.

Sarcococca ruscifolia or *S. confusa* is a simple little evergreen shrub, famous for its glossy leaves and the strong, sweet vanilla fragrance of its little white flowers. Add a few sprigs to every winter bouquet to scent the house.

Aucuba japonica 'Variegata' is a showy evergreen shrub with dark-green leaves splotched and spattered with sunny yellow.

Contorted hazelnut (*Corylus avellana* 'Contorta') has gnarled, twisted branches that look as if they had been caught in a cyclone. The fantastical bare branches add height and interest to any arrangement, and in spring they drip with long yellow catkins.

Witch hazel (*Hamamelis* ssp.) is one of the earliest blooming fragrant shrubs. 'Pallida' has bright-yellow fragrant flowers in midwinter; 'Jelena' has flowers of burnt orange. Any witch hazel with Chinese parentage is fragrant.

Salix caprea (French pink pussy willows) are ungainly shrubs, but the pink-gray, fat, woolly pussies (which dry beautifully) are worth the garden room.

Winter daphne (*Daphne ododora* 'Marginata') has evergreen leaves margined in creamy white and deliciously scented, long-lasting pink flowers.

Helleborus x *hybridus* is the rose of winter; its freckled and blotched blossoms come in white, yellow, shades of pink, and deepest purple.

EDIBLES FOR CUTTING

Bronze fennel, arugula and chive flowers, raspberries, cherry tomatoes, artichokes, cardoons, kale, and chard: choose any or all.

FOLIAGE FOR CUTTING

Magnolia grandiflora 'Little Gem' or 'Victoria' are the hardiest small evergreen magnolias with good indementum (copper fuzz) on the reverse side of the leaves.

Lamb's ear (*Stachys byzantina*) is a perennial with silver furry foliage and felted purple flower spike; it's drought tolerant.

Hostas are shade-loving perennials with large leaves in various textures. 'Sum and Substance' is the biggest and most chartreuse of the bunch; many are blue-toned or variegated. If leaves are a plant's lungs, hostas embody this notion in their generous, curved shape.

Granny's ringlets (*Cryptomeria japonica spiralis*) is a golden-green dwarf conifer with needles that grow in a distinct spiral pattern.

Senecio greyi is a small, tough shrub with pretty, gray-green leaves rimmed in silvery white that hold up year-round.

Heucheras are the ultimate little foliage perennial with scalloped leaves in colors from chartreuse 'Lime Rickey' to dark 'Chocolate Ruffles' to apricot 'Marmalade'.

Spirea japonica 'Magic Carpet' and 'Lime Mound' are small, deciduous shrubs with colored foliage.

Rosemary (*Rosmarinus officinalis*) is a bristly, fragrant-foliage shrub, as useful in the kitchen as in the garden and bouquets. It comes in various shapes (prostrate, upright) and is drought-tolerant and evergreen.

Bergenia spp. is also known as elephant's ears for the fat, paddle-shaped leaves that take on tints of red and bronze in winter. It has pink or purple spring-flower spikes.

Euphorbia spp. is consistent; even the chartreuse flowers look like foliage on this dependable perennial. *E.* 'Blackbird' with dark burgundy foliage and the fluffy little *E. dulcis* 'Chameleon' are favorites in bouquets over many months.

Epimedium spp. has evergreen, heart-shaped leaves on wiry stems that make this sturdy perennial a flower arranger's year-round dream plant.

Hedera helix 'Goldheart' or 'Buttercup' are two of the variegated, small-leafed ivies ideal for draping the sides of vases or winding through arrangements.

What to Grow

111

The Asiatic lily 'Tiny Orange Sensation' floats in a sea of 'Johnson's Blue' hardy geraniums in late July.

resources

I find my inspiration for bouquet-making in the natural world and in my own garden. I'm also influenced by art, interior design, travel, and garden design. Although there are many impressive books on floral design, few have anything to do with gardening, or with picking fresh flowers and bringing them indoors.

Because I was a horticultural librarian at the University of Washington for eighteen years, I can't help but share a few choice resources, both books and nurseries, that I hope help you enrich your garden and your bouquets.

Among web pages and blogs, I tend to browse among the most beautiful design, fashion, and gardening ones for visual inspiration. There are a few books that I turn to again and again, and I've listed these below.

If you'd like to keep up with my bouquet-making, you can see what is blooming in my garden and making it into new arrangements every week of the year on my blog, Plant Talk, at www.valeaston.com.

BOOKS

Several of the books are out-of-print, but should be available in libraries or used bookshops.

Color by Design: Planting the Contemporary Garden, Nori and Sandra Pope. SOMA Books, 1998.

The Flower Arranger's Garden, Rosemary Verey. Little, Brown and Co., 1989.

Fresh Cuts: Arrangements with Flowers, Leaves, Buds and Branches, Edwina von Gal. Artisan, 1997.

The Garden through the Year, Graham Stuart Thomas. Sagapress, Inc., 2002.

Right Plant, Right Place: Over 1,400 Plants for Every Situation in the Garden, Nicola Ferguson. Fireside, 2005.

The Wabi Sabi House: The Japanese Art of Imperfect Beauty, Robyn Griggs Lawrence. Clarkson Potter, 2004.

PLANTS

Fine mail-order nurseries and seed sources abound, and there are probably many small nurseries carrying interesting plants close to where you live. Here are a few websites and catalogs I couldn't garden without:

Annie's Annuals and Perennials, Richmond, CA, www.anniesannuals.com, 888-266-4370, has a lovely selection of temptingly unusual flowers, plus a free color catalog.

B&D Lilies, Port Townsend, WA, www.bdlilies.com, 360-765-4341, offers fabulously big and healthy Oriental, Asian, and Orienpet lilies, and also a gorgeous free catalog. This source alone will turn you into a lily connoisseur.

Brent and Becky's Bulbs, Gloucester, VA, www.brentandbeckysbulbs.com, 804-693-3966, is a source, I'm sure, for any and every bulb I've mentioned in this catalog, plus many more from this endlessly knowledgeable couple.

Joy Creek Nursery, Scapoose, OR, www.joycreek.com, 503-543-7474, proprietor Maurice Horn might specialize in gravel gardening, but his nursery is a treasure trove of clematis, hydrangea, fuchsia, and all manner of garden-worthy perennials, vines, and shrubs.

Plant Delights, Raleigh, NC, www.plantdelights.com, 919-772-4794, is the place for the coolest plants, the most unusual hostas and aroids; they'll send you a fabulously funny and engaging catalog for the asking.

Renee's Garden, Felton, CA, www.reneesgarden.com, 888-880-7228, has a fine selection of old-fashioned and heirloom sweet peas, cutting flowers, herbs, and vegetables; seeds are generally available at retail nurseries.

Territorial Seed Company, Cottage Grove, OR, www.territorialseed.com, 800-626-0866, is a reliable source that sells tried-and-true seeds and plants as well as the latest grafted varieties of vegetables; also flowers, herbs, and fruit.

White Flower Farm, Litchfield, CT, www.whiteflowerfarm.com, 800-503-9624, has the most beautiful reference-book of a catalog, and it's still free. The plants are big and healthy but pricey.

about the author

Photograph by Katie Easton

Valerie Easton started gardening to bring nature into the house, and she hasn't stopped planting, picking, and arranging flowers and foliage for the last forty years. Her new, simplified garden on Whidbey Island has been featured in *The New York Times*, *Horticulture*, and *This Old House*.

For eighteen years, Valerie worked as a horticultural librarian at the University of Washington. She hasn't missed a week of writing her "Plant Life" column for *Pacific Northwest Magazine* of the *Seattle Times* in the last fifteen years. She also writes feature articles for the *Times* on the region's most creative gardens and homes. She writes about gardens and the people who make them for numerous publications, including *Garden Design* and *Organic Gardening* magazines. Val is the author of four gardening books, including *The New Low Maintenance Garden*.

Valerie blogs at www.valeaston.com and for the Huffington Post, and teaches yoga in Langley, on Whidbey Island. She lives in Seattle and on Whidbey Island with her husband, Greg, and wheaten terrier, Bridget.